Tropical
Fruit
Cookbook

Tropical Fruit Cookbook

Marilyn Rittenhouse Harris

illustrated by

Charlene K. Smoyer

A Kolowalu Book

University of Hawaii Press

Honolulu

To my parents

©1993 University of Hawaii Press

All rights reserved

Printed in Singapore

98 97 96 95 94 93 5 4 3 2 1

Designed by Dana Levy, Perpetua Press

Library of Congress Cataloging-in-Publication Data

Harris, Marilyn R. (Marilyn Rittenhouse)

    Tropical fruit cookbook / Marilyn Rittenhouse Harris;
illustrated by Charlene K. Smoyer.

        p.   cm.

    "A Kolowalu book."

    Includes bibliographical references and index.

    ISBN 0-8248-1441-X

    1. Cookery (Tropical fruit)   I. Title.

TX811.H366   1993

641.6'46—dc20   92-44835

                                CIP

Contents

Preface

*L*USCIOUS TROPICAL FRUIT has had a special place in ceremony and symbolism beginning with Adam and Eve and Paradise. Even today with the continual encroachment of urbanization on all Hawaiian islands, there is the mirage of the banana patch and the recollection of a secret place to gather papayas, passion fruit, guavas, and wild mountain apples. The mystery continues to unfold as the bloom becomes the fruit and swells to maturity.

Most of the fruits arrived in Hawai'i after Captain Cook. Credited with introducing and producing a wide variety of fruit in Hawai'i is Don Francisco de Paula Marin, who knew Kamehameha I for more than twenty-five years. The Marin Gardens covered what is now Booth Park and the grounds of Pauoa Stream in lower Pauoa Valley on O'ahu. They had citrus, avocado, mango, Chinese plum, Tahitian wild apple, coffee, and Tahitian banana. Marin saw the early potential to fulfill the increasing demands for ships' supplies. The Islands were ideally located to supply China traders and the Pacific whaling fleet.

Today, pineapple makes up the bulk of farm fruit earnings with papaya a distant second followed by banana and guava. The tropical fruit industry is beginning to diversify, producing carambola, atemoya (commonly called "moya"), lychee, rambutan, and mango for the marketplace. For the backyard gardener, local nurseries carry a wide selection of tropical fruit trees.

Anyone interested in the nutritional or cookery aspects of tropical fruit in Hawai'i is indebted to early, well-educated, dedicated home economist pioneers. There was much curiosity about the nutritive values of tropical fruit compared with fruit grown in temperate climates. Professional home economists Carey Miller, Katherine Bazore Gruelle, Nao Wenkam, Mary Bartow, and Kathryn Orr conducted exacting nutritional studies on many local fruits. They gathered fruit samples throughout Hawai'i and tested them under state-of-the-art laboratory conditions. They laid a sound academic foundation that established the nutritive values for local tropical fruits. These pioneer economists developed recipes that appeared in books and pamphlets encouraging the use of local fruits. The original nutritional information giving composition of fruits grown in Hawai'i was first available in 1936 as *Some Fruits of Hawaii*, and subsequent bulletins were issued by the Hawaii Agricultural Experiment Station. In 1945, the forerunner of University of Hawaii Press published *Fruits of Hawaii* by Miller, Bazore, and Bartow. It has been reprinted through the years.

This book updates recipes for tropical fruit preparation consistent with contemporary life-styles and provides information on new market fruit. Current nutritional studies show that fruit is naturally low in calories, high in vitamins and minerals, and a good source of fiber. The Nutritional Value of Fruits table was prepared by Joda Derrickson, M.S., R.D., Nutritional Specialist, University of Hawaii at Mānoa.

The information on fruit trees, vines, and shrubs is included for general interest to the cook and backyard gardener. It is in no sense a botanical guide. I gratefully acknowledge the assistance of agricultural professionals Richard Yoshida, Frank Sekiya, Bob Hamilton, Eric Weinert, Jack Gushiken, Diane Ragone, Skip Bittenbender, Richard Manshardt, Nick Housego, and Mike Strong who have been patient and generous with their time.

I would like to thank my editor at University of Hawaii Press, who has been unobtrusive in her guidance, and my computer guru, Roger, who eased my way into an electronic manuscript. The librarians and staff at Midkiff Learning Center, The Kamehameha Schools; Hamilton Library at the University of Hawaii; the Hawaii State Public Library System; and the Bernice Pauahi Bishop Museum Library have shared their time and collections with me.

Thanks to my father and brother for their camaraderie in tramping the rainy fields of Hilo and Kona seeing and tasting the glorious tropical fruits. For their encouragement and expertise, I thank husband Chris and friends Lu, Margaret, Charlene, and Sigrid.

How to Use This Cookbook

*T*HE HISTORY, description, and recipes for more than forty common and not-so-common popular tropical fruits are included in the book. Information about the fruit is followed by appropriate recipes using microwave, stove top, and conventional oven cooking methods. Recipes are included for soups, salads, appetizers, entrées, chutney, salsa, fruit spreads, breads, and desserts. Some recipes will appeal to the gourmet cook, but most are simple and will suit a novice cook.

For best results, read the recipe carefully before starting to cook, checking the ingredients and equipment needed. If directions are not clear, consult the basic fruit cookery information that follows in this section. The book also includes tips on fast and easy ways to use tropical fruits, a nutrition table, and ideas for using a bumper crop of ripe fruit.

Recipes are, at best, suggestions. Creativity is the fun and excitement of cookery—the art or practice of preparing food. Cooking a good recipe is like making a fun, edible art form. I hope you will find some recipes in this book which will do that for you.

Basic Fruit Cookery

*C*OOKING FRUIT FOR any length of time dissipates its flavor. Retain 1 or 2 tablespoons of the fresh fruit juice or purée to add to the finished dish before serving. This intensifies the fruitiness of the dish. Recent studies indicate that four-fifths of a flavor is aroma, so the scent of the fruit augments its taste.

What Is Purée? Purée is obtained by mashing foodstuffs and can be done to fish, meat, vegetables, or fruit. Traditionally, it was done with a mortar and pestle. Today, a food processor fitted with a knife blade or a blender works well. The purée can be frozen at least nine months and should be frozen with no additions for maximum flexibility in recipes. Tropical fruit purées give a distinctive flavor and texture to marinades. Fruit purée is cooked for fruit butters but frequently is not cooked for dessert toppings and sauces. It can be sweetened with honey or liqueurs. Using fresh fruit purée rather than fruit juice in recipes adds fiber without added sugar. Substituting fruit juice in recipes calling for fruit purée may not give satisfactory results because the flavor, texture, and sweetness differ.

How to Shred Fruit The cheese grating knife of a food processor makes wonderful shredded green mango and green papaya. These fruit shreds are good for salsa, salad, relish, pickled dishes, and textured sauces. The fruit needs to be firm and not ripe to shred properly. Shredded mango and papaya freeze well for at least 6 months.

Tropical Fruit Jam or Fruit Spread Both traditional and freezer methods for making fruit jam use large amounts of sugar, about 1 cup of sugar or other sweetener to 1 cup of fruit. Newer methods employ various techniques to avoid large amounts of sugar, which mask the true flavor of the fruit. The desirable product is a spreadable fruit. It may require no sweetener. If a sweeter product is desired, concentrated fruit juice or a small amount of honey or sugar may be added.

One new method uses fruit pectin to make light jam or jelly with little or no sugar. Another contemporary method incorporates unflavored gelatin or agar for the jelling process. Gelatin cannot be used with fresh pineapple, papaya, or kiwi because they contain enzymes that break down the animal protein in gelatin and prevent jelling. Agar, a seaweed extract, can be substituted for gelatin and used to jell fresh pineapple, papaya, or kiwi. Agar is found in block, thread, or powder form and has been used in the Orient for centuries. Three tablespoons of agar flakes, one stick of agar, or 2 tablespoons of gelatin each jell approximately 4 cups of liquid purée or fruit pieces. Both the fruit pectin and agar or gelatin methods produce a fruit spread with a chunkier fruit texture, brighter color, and fresher fruit flavor than the traditional jam. They are cooked for short periods of time. These fruit spreads become spreadable fruit. They will be tart if the fruit is not sweet (pohā, guava). Honey can be added before serving or freezing for a sweeter product.

Fruit spreads should be stored in the freezer or refrigerator, never at room temperature. If they don't jell immediately, they will set up after chilling. The fruity taste, chunky texture, and nutritional aspects make these spreads outstanding.

Salsa

Enjoying new popularity, salsa is a familiar condiment with some new ingredients. It is low in fat, intensely flavored, and replaces high-calorie cream and butter sauces for beef, poultry, and fish. Salsa has a fresh flavor that may or may not be hot. A fruit-based salsa is tart, cool, and refreshing. The ingredients in a salsa are limited only by one's imagination. Ginger or a hot Chinese chili oil can be substituted for hot chili peppers. Onions provide a pungent flavor—yellow the strongest, next red, and scallions the mildest. Lime juice or fruit bits is the usual source of tartness for salsa, but tamarind concentrate, vinegar, pummelo juice or fruit bits, carambola juice or stars, or passion fruit juice or pulp can be used. Chinese parsley (cilantro) is the traditional herb used, but mint, parsley, or basil can be substituted. Salsa is a last-minute preparation not requiring accurate measurements. It keeps for at least 2 weeks under refrigeration.

Chutney

Chutney is a condiment of Indian origin. It consists of chopped fruit or vegetables cooked with spices, onion, garlic, chilies, vinegar, and sugar to the consistency of jam. In Hawai'i, green mango is the popular fruit for chutney; however, carambola, guava, kumquat, papaya, pineapple, pomegranate, tamarind, or a combination of fruit also make good chutney.

The cups of fruit and liquid given in chutney recipes are flexible. Most recipes work with slightly more or slightly less fruit. There are no fixed spices or ingredients for chutney. It is customarily prepared to personal taste. A variety of chutneys including sweet, sour, spicy, and mild can be used in appetizer, entrée, and dessert recipes. The popular use for chutney is a condiment with curry, but chutney can add a unique flavor to marinade, barbecue sauce, and salad dressing.

What Is Zest?

Many fruit spreads, baking recipes, and chutney list zest as an ingredient. It is the outermost part of the rind of citrus fruit, grated to add piquancy to food. A zester is the most efficient tool for making the tiny aromatic strands of citrus peel that also lend texture, color, and flavor to food. Store lemon, lime, pummelo, grapefruit, tangerine, and orange rinds in the freezer. Grate as needed for recipes.

Tropical Fruit Bread

Fruit bread, typically moist and rich with fiber and nutrients, is a healthful addition to a diet. For best results, drain chopped or sliced fruit thoroughly. A salad spinner is useful for this task.

A bread containing uniform fruit pieces under one-half inch bakes more evenly than one with larger chunks of fruit. Fruit purée bakes well in bread, but when converting a recipe to include fruit pieces or fruit purée, it may be necessary to reduce the amount of liquid used in the dough and to adjust flour or cereal accordingly. If a fruit bread is damp after baking, remove it from the pan and return the bread to the oven for a few minutes with the oven turned off.

Most tropical fruits can be used in muffins, breads, pancakes, and waffles. The more exotic fruits like 'ōhelo or pohā can be used like cranberry or cherry. Passion fruit, pomegranate, banana, and persimmon can be used as a purée. Papaya, mango, lychee, guava, citrus, pineapple, and carambola can be coarsely chopped or puréed. Two or more fruits can be blended. For example, banana blends well with pineapple or carambola; passion fruit with lychee; and pomegranate with mango or papaya.

Tips for Making Tropical Fruit Quick Breads This type of bread has a distinctive ingredient: baking powder. It makes them easy to mix and eliminates rising time. To be effective, baking powder must be fresh. Check the expiration date. If there is no date or if near expiration, add a teaspoon of baking powder to $1/2$ cup of hot water. The mixture should foam. If it doesn't foam, don't use the baking powder. Throw it away.

Add 1 teaspoon guava, mango, papaya, pineapple, or passion fruit jam to half-full muffin tins. Cover with batter to two-thirds full. Place 1 tablespoon puréed fruit on top of bread or muffin batter before baking.

Many prepared muffin or bread mixes provide instructions for the addition of fruit to the batter. Add well-drained tropical fruit cut to a uniform size.

Fresh fruit tidbits are best added to pancakes on the griddle just after the dough sets. Fruit tidbits give a more intense flavor to pancakes than purée. Banana, papaya, pineapple, mango, and lychee are good.

Flavored Butter Use with coffee cake, pancakes, muffins, and specialty bread. Whip softened butter or margarine and flavor it with mashed guava, mango, persimmon, or pineapple or with lemon, orange, tangerine, or lime zest. Fruit chutney is also good. Use one part chutney or mashed fruit to two parts softened butter or margarine.

Tropical Fruit Salad The desire to watch calories and to eat healthful food has increased the popularity of salads. Their role in a balanced diet is enlarged, and it is not unusual to see salad featured as a main entrée.

Look for color combinations when composing a salad. Imagine how green avocado, pink guava, red pomegranate seeds, yellow star fruit (carambola), or bright orange will look in a salad. Put together a variety of textures and tastes—juicy, smooth, crisp, tart, and sweet. A salad spinner will dry greens thoroughly and remove excess liquid from fruits. Use only fresh greens and do not dress them until ready to serve, or allow guests to control the amount of dressing on their salads by serving the dressing separately. Conversely, when combining fruit flavors for a combination salad or making a breadfruit salad, similar to potato salad, be sure to allow ample time for the mixture to chill in the marinade or dressing for best results.

Tropical Fruit Soups

Fruit soups are traditionally placed among exotic foods and are not served as frequently as they deserve. Fruit purée is easily turned into a simple fruit soup with the addition of yogurt, milk, fruit juice, or sweet or dry wine. These fruits are exceptionally good to purée for soups: avocado, guava, mango, moya, papaya, passion fruit, persimmon, pineapple, and pomegranate. The flavors of two or three fruits can be blended for a combination soup. For example, carambola or moya blend well with avocado, papaya, mango, or persimmon. Lychee juice is good with guava, passion fruit, or pineapple. Spirits like sherry, dark rum, and kirsch enrich the fruit flavor. This type of fruit soup is best served chilled or even frozen and served slightly slushy. For breakfast or brunch, an avocado soup is both more substantial and more interesting than plain fruit or fruit juice.

Fruit soups can be served at a brunch with small rolls, biscuits, and other finger foods. For luncheons, fruit soups are nutritious and can be hearty. Many fruit soups make elegant and simple desserts served with cookies or a selection of cheeses. With a change of spice or other ingredient, the fruit soup can fit into many occasions.

Fruited Ice Creams

Most ice cream freezers carry manufacturer's instructions for making fruit ice cream and these are generally appropriate for tropical fruits. Be sure to drain the fruit and to cook the egg custard base adequately to avoid any danger of salmonella. Do not use uncooked egg white in the final preparation.

An easy way to have a tropical fruit ice cream is to add the fruit to commercial ice creams. This provides an endless variety of flavors. The resulting ice cream gives the original product more flavor, nutrients, texture, and color. The end result is often a better flavor than the commercial tropical fruit ice cream. It is possible to please those who are diet conscious by selecting an ice milk or sherbet for a base. If a rich, creamy dessert is appropriate, select a gourmet ice cream. Be adventurous and experiment with unusual combinations. Combine chocolate ice cream with lychee; guava purée with watermelon sherbet; or passion fruit, including seeds, with strawberry ice cream.

Flavors of ice cream intensify if frozen 24 hours before serving. This applies to both homemade ice cream and to commercial ice cream to which fruit is added.

Basic Sorbet or Granita

Two cups of fruit purée make four servings. Choose one or a blend of fruits: carambola, tangerine, pummelo, orange, guava, lychee, mango, moya, papaya, persimmon, pineapple, pomegranate, passion fruit, or tamarind (use $1/3$ cup tamarind concentrate with 2 cups water). For a dessert sorbet, sweeten with 1 tablespoon honey. Do not sweeten for an appetizer or palate refresher. With bland fruits, such as papaya or persimmon, supplement with 1 tablespoon lime juice. Blend purée with sweetener. Chill thoroughly. Pour mixture into divided ice-cube trays or into an 8-inch-square pan. Freeze until almost firm. Place four or five cubes at a time into processor bowl, or break mixture into large pieces and place into processor bowl. Process several seconds with knife blade until fluffy but not thawed. Spoon sorbet into individual serving dishes and refreeze until firm. Sorbet should have the consistency of coarse snow when served.

This frozen treat, which does not contain milk or egg white as sherbet does, is well suited to today's light cuisine. Traditionally, sorbet is served between courses to cleanse the palate, but it can be used as an appetizer and as a refreshing dessert. It is good topped with slices of fresh tropical fruit. Sorbet is best mixed smooth in a food processor or blender after freezing and then immediately refrozen before serving.

The Italian version, granita, is coarser than the French sorbet. It is not stirred during or after the freezing process to preserve its rough texture. Place cubes directly into serving containers and gently break up before serving.

Tips for Making Sorbet and Granita Chill ingredients before freezing to improve the icy consistency. Cover sorbet and granita in the refrigerator or freezer so they do not pick up flavors from other foods or moisture, which makes them sticky.

Sorbet can become too crystalline if left in the freezer for several days. To restore it, partially thaw the sorbet and process again in food processor or blender. Refreeze and use within 24 hours.

Tropical Fruit Ice Blocks Be sure the mold fits into the freezer and that it is no larger than the punch bowl before beginning. An ice block or cubes made from moya purée adds a unique tartness to any fruit punch. Muffin tins can be used to make large-size cubes. Canned concentrated, frozen tropical fruit juice (passion fruit or guava) can be used in small punch bowls as an ice block and it provides an additional flavor.

To make a tropical fruit ice ring for a punch bowl, overlap thin slices of fruit, one kind or a mixture, in the bottom of a ring mold. Choose from carambola, mango, orange, papaya, pineapple, or tangerine and include thin slices of lime or lemon. Pour one-fourth inch water over the fruit and freeze until solid. Fill remaining space with water and freeze. Unmold and float the ice fruit side up in the punch.

Tropical Fruit in Cakes The addition of fruit to a packaged cake mix can be done successfully with these proportions: substitute 1 cup drained and diced fruit for 1/4 cup water and follow directions on the package for a tube-pan cake. These fruits go well with a white or a yellow cake mix: lychee, mango, papaya, and pineapple. The addition of coconut extract to replace vanilla or almond in a cake batter provides another tropical flavor, especially if it is repeated in the frosting.

Fruit Leather Rolled sheets of dried fruits have been sold in food markets for several years. They are flavorful and chewy, a perfect snack.

There are several ways to prepare fruit leather. Using the sun's heat for drying can be a time-consuming process requiring cloudless, sunny, and dry weather. It may take 20–24 hours for the leather to dry depending on the type of fruit and the sun's heat.

There are several alternatives to sun drying. Oven drying requires temperatures between 130° and 150°, which are unavailable in many ovens. Drying in an electric dehydrator often produces the best-quality product. It represents an initial investment, and its construction, ease of operation, warranty, and frequency of use should be considered.

The microwave is another possibility for making fruit leather. This is a basic microwave recipe for making fruit leather; it may require adjustment depending on the variable water content of the fruit. It may be necessary to increase or to decrease cooking time. Use ¾ cup fruit purée. Line a 14 by 11 by 2-inch microwave-safe container with parchment paper. Pour in fruit purée. Cook at High 11 minutes and at Medium 3 minutes. Remove and let stand until cool and dry. Cut into strips.

Bulk Use for Tropical Fruit

There are times when too much tropical fruit is at hand to eat. Tropical fruit ice cubes are a good way to store extra purée. Cubes can be used in ice tea, mineral water, daiquiris, margaritas, sparklers, or put into a blender or food processor for smoothies. Make ice cubes in divided trays with fruit purée. Freeze in plastic bags or freezer containers.

To use up a bumper crop of tropical fruit, make fruit spreads, chutney, salsa, breads, fruit leather, salad dressings, fruitsicles, barbecue sauce, fruit catsup, and marinades. Fruit can also be added to commercial ice cream and sherbet and refrozen.

Island-Style Cooking

In Hawai'i, Island- or Pacific-style cooking is popular. It requires some ingredients and seasonings for which there are no satisfactory substitutes. Omissions may result in a dish lacking the necessary character. For this type of food preparation, locate an Asian market for oyster sauce, hoisin sauce, rice vinegar, Chinese chili sauce, light and dark soy sauce, Chinese parsley (cilantro), gingerroot, and tamarind concentrate if the supermarket does not have the ingredients.

Gingerroot is a basic ingredient and is used in most cuisines of the world because of its unique tingly, fresh, hot flavor. Ginger may be found dried, candied, or preserved. Gingerroot is knobby, firm, and gray-beige. Peel the fresh root and cut in thin slices that fit into a garlic press. Load the press with small batches and press to obtain fiber-free ginger juice. Remove and discard pulp after each pressing. Ginger juice is easily dispersed throughout the food, allowing the flavor to permeate the dish. Another method is to place thin ginger slices in a food processor and use a knife blade to mince it. A third method is to use a porcelain grater to grate the fresh gingerroot finely. Gingerroot pieces or juice can be frozen without damaging its potency. Neither commercial ground ginger nor crystallized ginger is a suitable substitute for gingerroot.

Avocado

Persea americana

*T*HE SPANISH HORTICULTURIST Don Francisco de Paula Marin fought for Kamehameha I and remained in Hawai'i from 1793 to 1826. During his residency, he introduced many valuable plants from various countries of the world to Hawai'i. The first avocado trees were in his gardens in Pauoa Valley on O'ahu, located mauka of Punchbowl Crater between Makiki and Pacific Heights. In 1825, when the H.M.S. *Blonde* returned to the Islands from England bearing the bodies of Kamehameha II and Queen Kamāmalu, a naturalist aboard made a journal entry noting that avocado plants were already in Hawai'i.

Avocado, from the Spanish *aguacate*, has been known by many names throughout history. "Alligator pear" appeared in 1669 and refers to the fruit's texture and shape. The avocado, native to tropical America, appears in an Aztec hieroglyphic about 291 B.C. describing the location of *ahuacatl* (avocado) trees. The Aztecs considered avocado an aphrodisiac. Recent unconfirmed reports tell about the successful use of avocado as an aphrodisiac by lower Amazon Basin tribes who prefer the fruit to more readily available marijuana.

Avocado is an evergreen tree forty to eighty feet tall related to the bay, laurel, camphor, and cinnamon trees. Avocado trees may live for a century, but most bear for about 25 years beginning at 4–8 years. A good tree can give 500 fruits a season—some trees bear 1,200–3,000.

The tiny flowers are green-yellow on four- to eight-inch branch tips. The three horticultural avocado varieties are Guatemalan (rough, woody skin), West Indian (smooth, thin, leathery skin), and Mexican (thin skin and spice-scented leaves). The green skin can change to red, purple, or purple-black as the fruit matures.

The fruit is pear-shaped or round, contains a single large seed, and weighs from one-fourth pound to three pounds. The golden green to pale yellow flesh is smooth and velvety with a slightly nutty, delicate flavor. Avocado ripens after it is picked, not while it is on the tree. Mature fruit, when full size, may change color or lose glossiness and when cut should reveal a brown seed coat. Fruit ripens better and is less likely to spoil if picked with the stem intact rather than pulled from the branch without a stem. Store fruit at room temperature approximately 10 days to ripen. To retard ripening, green, mature fruit can be stored in the refrigerator for 2 weeks before beginning the ripening process. To hasten ripening, put avocados in a paper bag and seal. An avocado is ripe when it yields to gentle pressure.

In Hawai'i, the thin-skinned West Indian variety produces best below 1,000 feet elevation, but the Guatemalan and Mexican hybrids will tolerate the cooler conditions of 2,000–2,500 feet elevation. Some trees bear in the fall and winter, others bear in winter and spring, with the summer crop smallest. Kona, on the island of Hawai'i, both at sea level and up to an elevation of 1,600 feet, produces magnificent avocados.

Use

Avocado is a healthful tropical fruit. It contains seventeen vitamins and minerals and has more potassium than many other fruits and vegetables. Avocado has a high percentage of protein and contains no cholesterol.

Preparing an avocado is easy. Cut it lengthwise around the seed and rotate the halves to separate. Remove the seed by sliding the tip of a spoon underneath or carefully hit the seed with the edge of a sharp knife and rotate the knife to lift out the seed. To peel, place the cut side down and remove the skin either with a knife or with fingers. To slice, lay the peeled avocado half cut-side down and slice into crescents. For avocado rings, cut fruit in half crosswise. Avocados darken quickly when sliced, but dipping them into lime or lemon juice, cider, or wine vinegar will retard the discoloration.

Avocado pulp can be frozen for up to 6 months. Mash the pulp and mix in 2–3 tablespoons of lime or lemon juice per avocado. Store in a freezer bag or an air-tight container. Use frozen pulp in sandwich spreads, guacamole and other dips, molded salads, scrambled eggs or omelets, ice cream, or sherbet. Ripe avocados can be stored in the refrigerator about 1 week.

Although botanically it is a fruit, the avocado can be prepared as a vegetable. It combines well with beef, poultry, seafood, rice, pasta, and potatoes. Avocado should be added in the last few minutes of cooking or broiled quickly in the oven. If cooked at a high temperature, it becomes bitter.

To grow an avocado seed, wash and remove the pulp and any brown seed coat. Form a tripod with three toothpicks, inserting them into the seed one-third up from the large end. Fill a jar or glass with water to cover half the seed. Stand the seed, pointed end up, in the water, keeping one-half inch of the seed wet. Set in a warm location away from direct sunlight. Add water as needed to sustain level. The seed should sprout within 6 weeks. When the stem reaches six inches, prune to three inches for additional growth. When the stem has leaves and several roots, plant it into a ten-inch pot using a potting mixture. Leave the top half of the seed exposed. Water when dry and feed with plant food for abundant leaves. Prune frequently to encourage more branches. This is an attractive house plant, but do not expect it to fruit. To obtain avocado fruit from a plant, buy a hybrid because the product from seed is variable.

Avocado Tips

When avocados are plentiful, it is sometimes a challenge not to waste any.

* Use mashed avocado as a topping for baked potatoes. Mash one avocado with 3 tablespoons of plain yogurt to top four baked potatoes.

* Avocado halves provide an ideal edible container. Stuff them with potato salad, chili, fruit, gelatin salad, sherbet, scrambled eggs, or light sour cream and caviar.

* Use guacamole to top chili, hamburgers, pizza; and to stuff mushroom caps, tacos, and omelets. Serve guacamole as an accompaniment for Mexican dishes, grilled beef, poultry, and seafood.

* Avocado slices or chunks can be added to a warm pasta or rice dish just before serving or tossed with the other ingredients in a cold pasta or rice salad.

* Mashed or puréed avocado added to French, thousand island, green goddess, and ranch-style salad dressings makes them creamy and rich tasting.

✳   Avocado can be used to thicken soups and to provide an interesting new flavor. Add $1/2$ cup puréed avocado to 1 can prepared soup during the last minutes of cooking. Warm avocado, but do not boil. Clam chowder, cream of mushroom or cream of chicken, potato, and tomato bisque are good combinations with avocado. To 1 can prepared tomato soup, add $1/2$ cup puréed avocado, $1/4$ cup minced cucumber, and $1/4$ cup minced green onion.

✳✳✳✳✳✳✳

Tropical Avocado Dip

Yield: 3 cups

2   cups avocado chunks

$1/2$ cup pineapple chunks

$1/4$ cup plain yogurt

$1/2$ cup low-cholesterol mayonnaise

1   tablespoon finely chopped mint or 1 tablespoon minced dill weed

Purée all ingredients to a chunky consistency using the knife blade in a blender or food processor. Cover and chill at least 1 hour to blend flavors.

Use the chilled dip with chips and cut vegetables or serve it at room temperature as a sauce over cooked asparagus or carrots.

Variation: 1 cup drained tofu can be substituted for the yogurt and mayon-

Island-Style Avocado Cocktail

Yield: 3 dozen balls

1/2 cup olive oil

3 tablespoons passion fruit pulp, juice, or lime juice

2 tablespoons dark rum

2 garlic cloves, crushed

1 teaspoon sesame seeds

2 large, firm, ripe avocados

Cocktail picks

Whisk together the marinade ingredients in a medium bowl. Cut avocados lengthwise and remove pulp with a melon-ball cutter. Place avocado balls in the marinade, cover, and chill at least 4 hours. Drain and insert a cocktail pick into each avocado ball.

Variation: Add 1/8 teaspoon sesame oil to marinade ingredients.

Tip: After removing avocado balls from marinade, whisk 1/4 cup yogurt or imitation sour cream into the marinade and refrigerate. Use as a salad dressing or as a sauce for vegetables.

Guacamole

Yield: 4 cups

The texture of guacamole can be varied by the amount of mashing of the avocado pulp. For a smooth consistency, use a blender or food processor to purée the avocado. For a chunky dip, leave the avocado in large pieces.

3 ripe avocados

1 teaspoon lime juice

1/2 cup minced onion

2 garlic cloves, crushed

1/4 cup plain yogurt, low-cholesterol mayonnaise, or sour cream

1/4 cup chopped green chilies or bottled chili pepper sauce to taste

1/2 cup diced tomato

Combine all ingredients except diced tomato in food processor container or medium mixing bowl. Process with metal blade or mix by hand or with electric mixer to desired consistency. Fold in diced tomato, spoon into serving container, and offer assorted cut vegetables or chips.

Variation: Garnish with minced Chinese parsley (cilantro) or pomegranate seeds; stir 1/4 cup drained pineapple tidbits into guacamole before serving.

Avocado Salad Dressing

Yield: 3 cups

2   cups avocado purée
1   cup buttermilk
1   garlic clove, crushed
2   teaspoons lemon juice
2   teaspoons mashed anchovy fillets
2   ounces blue cheese
1   teaspoon Worcestershire sauce
1   teaspoon coarsely ground pepper

Mix all ingredients in blender or food processor container to a smooth consistency. Chill thoroughly before serving. This dressing is especially good on seafood salads and vegetables.

Toasted Seafood Avocado

Yield: 4 servings

4   ripe, firm avocados
1   cup cooked crab, imitation crab, or lobster chunks
2   tablespoons orange juice or lychee juice
2   tablespoons blue cheese or ranch-style salad dressing
1/4 cup diced lychee, mango, or pineapple

Topping:
1/2 cup process cheese
2   tablespoons coarsely chopped macadamia nuts

Wash fruit thoroughly and cut lengthwise, removing the pit. If necessary, flatten the base for stability by removing a small amount of skin, but don't cut through. Remove the pulp with a spoon, leaving shells intact. Place avocado pulp into a medium bowl and mash to a coarse consistency. Add seafood, fruit juice, and salad dressing. Mix well. Fold in fruit pieces and fill shells. Blend cheese topping with nuts. Spoon topping over avocado shells and broil quickly in the oven to warm. High or prolonged heat to avocado may result in a bitter taste. Serve immediately.

Burritos Island Style

1   ounce dried shiitake mushrooms

2   cups hot water

2   green onions, chopped

1   teaspoon finely minced ginger-
    root

2   cups shredded Chinese cabbage
    (won bok)

1   cup shredded carrot

1/2 cup shredded cucumber

2   tablespoons low-sodium soy sauce

1   tablespoon arrowroot blended
    with 2 tablespoons water

2   cups shredded imitation crab or
    lobster

12 (6-inch) flour tortillas

6   tablespoons hoisin sauce blended
    with 6 tablespoons water

Sauce:

2   cups avocado purée

1/2 cup imitation sour cream or plain
    yogurt

Lightly coat a wok or skillet with vegetable cooking spray. Soak mushrooms in hot water 15 minutes, drain, and discard water. Cut mushrooms into julienne strips; set aside. Place prepared wok or skillet over medium heat. Add onions and gingerroot and sauté 1 minute before adding cabbage, carrot, cucumber, and soy sauce. Stir-fry 2 minutes. Add arrowroot mixture to vegetables; mix. Cook, stirring constantly, until thickened, about 2 minutes. Stir in mushrooms and shredded crab. Do not overcook. Warm tortillas according to package instructions. Spread 1 tablespoon hoisin sauce mixture over each tortilla. Place 1/2 cup crab mixture down the center of each tortilla and roll up. Combine avocado sauce ingredients. Spoon avocado sauce over burritos. Serve with pineapple salsa.

Avocado Sorbet

Yield: 6 servings

3 large avocados

¼ cup lime juice

⅛ teaspoon bottled chili pepper sauce or to taste

2 tablespoons celery seeds

¼ cup minced tomato

1 tablespoon onion flakes

Garnish: Thin slices of avocado

Peel and coarsely chop avocados. Place in food processor container; add lime juice and chili pepper sauce. Process with knife blade for 1 minute or until mixture is smooth. Blend in celery seeds, minced tomato, and onion flakes. Chill thoroughly. Pour mixture into divided ice cube trays or into an 8-inch-square pan. Freeze until almost firm. Place four or five cubes at a time into processor container or break mixture into large pieces and place in processor. Use knife blade and process until fluffy but not thawed. Spoon mixture into serving dishes and refreeze until firm. Sorbet should have the consistency of coarse snow when served. Garnish each serving with two or three very thin avocado slices. Use as a first course served with a cheese cracker or chutney biscuit.

Avocado Soup I

Yield: 4 ½ cups

2 cups avocado purée

½ cup pineapple juice

1 cup carrot purée

1 cup papaya or lemon yogurt

1 teaspoon nutmeg

Garnish: 2 teaspoons paprika

Thoroughly mix all ingredients. Pour into individual soup bowls and garnish. Best served at room temperature.

Fruit Basket Party Salad

Yield: 16 servings

2   (6-ounce) packages strawberry
     gelatin
4   cups boiling water
1   cup cold water
1   cup passion-orange juice or
     orange juice
2   cups 1/2-inch avocado chunks
1   (20-ounce) can crushed pine-
     apple, undrained
2   cups lychee halves, drained
2   tablespoons orange zest
1/4 cup water
1/4 cup passion fruit pulp with seeds
     or lemon juice
1   envelope unflavored gelatin
16 ounces low-fat lemon yogurt

Combine the gelatin and boiling water in one 13 by 9-inch or two 10 by 6-inch glass containers and mix well to blend. Add the cold water and the fruit juice. Stir in the avocado chunks, pineapple, lychees, and zest. Chill overnight or 3–4 hours to set.

Combine water, passion fruit pulp, and unflavored gelatin in a small pan. Allow gelatin to soften and then cook over medium heat, stirring to dissolve completely. Remove from heat. Combine yogurt with the gelatin mixture and beat until smooth. Cool slightly before pouring yogurt mixture over chilled strawberry gelatin. Chill salad 2 hours or until set. Cut into squares. This layered molded salad is lovely for a shower or bridal luncheon.

Avocado Soup II

Yield: 4 cups

2   cups avocado purée
1   cup pummelo or grapefruit purée
1/4 cup minced watercress
1   cup banana yogurt
Garnish: Watercress leaves

Thoroughly mix all ingredients. Pour into individual soup bowls and garnish. Best served chilled.

Banana

Musa paradisiaca

THE BANANA PLANT, the largest herb in the world, can rise forty feet from base to crown. The banana is a berry originally containing numerous hard seeds and historians speculate that its root was the edible portion. It has been cultivated for at least 10,000–15,000 years. Early man propagated the species to give more fruit and less seeds, hence the seedless banana. Distant relatives of the banana are the orchid, garden lily, and palm. It is named for Antonius Musa, a physician to Octavius Augustus, first emperor of Rome, 63 B.C.–A.D.14.

From its origin in the Asian tropics, the Arabs carried the banana to Africa and to the Canary Islands, from which the Portuguese or Spanish took it to the New World. The banana has captured the imagination of man throughout history in legends, religious practices, and music. Westerners first saw the banana in 327 B.C. when Alexander the Great reached the Indus Valley. In the Koran, the banana plant is the "Tree of Paradise" and its leaves were used by Adam and Eve to cover their bodies, certainly more appropriately than the small fig leaf. During the Middle Ages, the banana was called the "apple of paradise"; thus, the modern confusion of pictures showing Eve offering Adam a red apple. The banana made its commercial entry into the United States at the 1876 Philadelphia Exposition and soon became a staple in American households.

In contemporary times, the banana is linked with humor. "Just because you have a nose like a banana doesn't mean you're one of the bunch." Someone "goes bananas." Hollywood has had a long love affair with the banana. There is "Yes, We Have No Bananas" and "Mellow Yellow." Woody Allen's first film was *Bananas*.

There are about 300 varieties of banana—tall plants and dwarf ones divided equally between sweet dessert types and starchy vegetable types. The fruits vary in size, color, shape, quantity, and quality. They can be short and round or long and skinny in red, yellow, or green.

Half the total world banana production is eaten raw and the remainder is cooked. Bananas are the third largest export of Iceland, where the fruit grows in greenhouses heated by water from volcanic underground springs.

This gigantic herb's trunk has no woody features but is actually tightly compressed layers of leaves. The Hawaiians said of a weakling, *He pūmai'a ia kanaka, he wale* (Falls easily as a banana stalk). The true stem of the herb is an underground rhizome whose large roots can cover thirty yards. Within nine to twelve months after planting, the banana attains 90 percent of its height and is ready to bear. The purple-red flower bud pushes through the leaves and as the bananas form, the blossom opens toward the ground. An upright blossom and fruit branches are found in Tahiti, Fiji, and other South Pacific islands. The dark purple blossom of the banana may be boiled or baked. It has a soft texture and a bittersweet taste. Banana flowers are eaten in some countries, cooked in coconut milk or pickled. If allowed to mature, the blossom fruits within 2–3 months.

The flowers develop into a "bunch" of bananas; each row of fruit is a "hand"; each fruit is a "finger." The bunch can be harvested when the fingers turn light green and the corners of the fruit are rounded rather than sharp. Bunches should be picked when fully developed but still green. Avoid the sap from the skin, stem leaves, or trunk of the plant because it is indelible and was even used as a dye by early Hawaiians. The fruit should be hung upside down in a cool, dark place to mature. A bunch of bananas can consist of 200 bananas and weigh seventy to eighty pounds. The banana produces only one bunch, and after the fruit is picked the plant is cut down. However, the plant has already put out shoots, called *keiki* (children) in Hawai'i, from its underground stem. In this manner, a banana plant may continue to produce for 60 years or longer.

More than seventy varieties of banana were known to the early Hawaiians, who undoubtedly brought bulblike rhizomes with them in their early and subsequent migrations. All but three varieties of bananas were forbidden fruit for Hawaiian women. The Hawaiians considered the time of day and the phase of the moon very important when planting bananas. The most favored time of day was high noon when the shadow "rested within the plant."

Of the early plants, the *hāpai* (pregnant) is one of the more interesting. The bananas mature two-thirds of the way up and inside the banana trunk. Ripeness is detected by swarming fruit flies or ants. Almost all the early types of bananas were cooked. They were steamed in an *imu* (underground oven), mashed into a *poi*, or roasted in hot ashes. Certain sweet varieties were used as a *pūpū* (appetizer) by *'awa* drinkers to quell the bitter taste.

A beautiful native banana is the *koa'e* (tropic bird), which has striped leaves and can be found near Kona. Nowadays, it is mainly sold as an ornamental because it produces few fruits. The major groups of bananas grown in Hawai'i both commercially and by backyard garden- ers are Bluefields, Brazilian (erroneously called "apple"), and Cavendish (which includes Chinese, a dwarf Cavendish brought to Hawai'i in 1855 from Tahiti; Williams Hybrid; and Valery).

Use

Bananas are found in three stages of ripeness—green tips, all yellow, and yellow with brown flecks. The riper the banana, the more nutritious and easily digestible it is. The indigestible starches in the green, raw state are eliminated by cooking or ripening. During the ripening process, the natural enzymes change the starches into sugars and make the banana soft and palatable. The strings clinging to the flesh contain tannin, are not sweet, and should be removed before eating. If the banana peel has no sheen or if the fruit feels soft, the banana was incorrectly ripened and may be mealy or tasteless. A quality banana should have a peel free of blemish, be plump, and have a shiny skin.

Bananas are good eaten raw, broiled, grilled, baked, and cooked in the peel in a microwave. Although bananas have the most flavor at room temperature, refrigerating a banana does not damage the texture of the flesh, but it does blacken the peel. When a banana reaches the desired ripeness, it can be refrigerated for 3–5 days. Overripe bananas can be used in smoothies, cakes, jams, ice cream, and bread. Banana purée can be frozen with 1 teaspoon lemon juice per cup of purée for up to 6 months.

Plantain

A plantain (cooking banana) looks like an oversize or jumbo banana. It is a staple food in many countries and is called the "potato of the tropics." It is firm, starchy, and dense, with three to four clearly defined sides. The skin varies from reddish brown to black, green, or yellow. Plantain peel is tougher than a banana peel, and the flesh is unaffected if the peel is blemished. As plantains ripen, they become softer. Plantains can be cooked at different stages of ripeness and are not usually eaten raw. Green plantains ripen at room temperature in 5–7 days.

An unripe, green plantain is slightly starchy and rather bland, similar to a potato. A half-ripe plantain is yellow or brown, comparable to a sweet potato with a creamy texture and a slight banana scent. A black plantain is ripe and has a slight banana taste. If the plantain turns black but remains hard, do not use it. When fully ripened and cooked, the sweetness of a ripe plantain can surpass that of a raw banana.

Green plantains are used in many cooked dishes—grated in soups, stews, and curries as a thickener and as a vegetable accompaniment to beef, poultry, and seafood. Their sweet starch is a good accompaniment to spicy barbecue items, stews, Mexican dishes, or curries. Boil, bake, grill, or whip them. Unpeeled plantains cook very well in the microwave. When soft to the touch, they are done. Very green plantains can be used for chips, comparable to thick potato chips. Plantains freeze well. When at desired ripeness, peel and wrap in freezer wrap. They will keep at least 3 months.

Peeling a raw plantain can be difficult, although the peel of a cooked fruit slides off easily. There are several ways to peel a raw plantain. One way is to cut off both end tips and then make a lengthwise cut down one of the ridges without piercing the pulp. Repeat on the adjacent ridge, cutting off one side of the peel. Lift off the top part of the section and pull down sharply. The entire segment of the peel should come off in one piece. Repeat for the other sides. Another method for peeling a raw plantain is to slice off both tips and cut it crosswise into halves. Make four lengthwise cuts along the ridges in each half. Pull away the peel crosswise rather than down.

Plantain Tips

✳ When soft, plantains are ready to eat. Select plantains that have a brown to black skin for best flavor or ripen a green plantain in about a week.

✳ To grill: Place an unpeeled plantain over medium coals until the skin is black and splitting slightly. The plantain should feel soft. Allow one-half plantain per serving.

✳ To microwave: Cook unpeeled plantains in the microwave at High for 5 minutes or until tender.

✳ To bake in the oven: Cook unpeeled plantains at 350° for 15 minutes or until tender.

✳ To use the plantain for dessert: After cooking in the peel, slit it and top with 1 teaspoon brown sugar and a dash of cinnamon. Or add 1 tablespoon dark rum to the slit plantain. Serve in the peel.

✳ To use the plantain for a vegetable: Cooked, mashed plantain can be formed into ½ inch balls and added to soups or stews during the last 3 minutes of cooking.

✳ Use cooked, yellow- or brown-skinned plantain as a potato substitute in omelettes or grated as hash brown potatoes.

✳✳✳✳✳✳

Easy Zippy Plantain

Select a brown- or black-skinned plantain, allowing one-half plantain per serving. Peel it and slice in one-fourth inch slices. Lightly coat a skillet with vegetable cooking spray and cook the plantain slices until golden, about 4 minutes per side. Season with salt and pepper and serve warm with chilled fruit salsa or spicy chutney dip.

Crispy Plantain

Yield: 4 servings

2   black, ripe plantains

1   egg white mixed with 1 table-spoon water

1   cup crushed whole-grain breakfast cereal

Peel plantains and slice crosswise in half and then lengthwise to make quarters. Dip slices into the egg white mixture. Coat with crumbs and bake 20 minutes at 350° until tender with a crispy crust.

Banana Smoothie

Begin the morning or end a workout with an icy cold shake. Yogurt and tropical fruit are a nutritious combination. Use frozen fruit for a thick smoothie. Best results are obtained when all ingredients, as well as the serving container, are chilled and the fruit is frozen.

1   (8-ounce) carton piña colada or banana yogurt

2   cups frozen banana chunks

1/2   cup guava juice or passion fruit juice

1   cup skim milk

1   cup frozen papaya, mango, or pineapple chunks

Ice cubes

Combine all ingredients except ice cubes in container of food processor or blender. Mix to a slushy consistency. Add enough ice cubes to make four servings and blend to smooth. Serve in chilled glasses.

Add one of these for a special smoothie:

1 teaspoon peanut butter per serving

Dash of cinnamon or nutmeg

1/4 teaspoon flavoring per serving (coconut, peppermint, almond, or vanilla)

Simple Banana Sauce

Yield: 1 cup

Juice of 1/2 lime

1   teaspoon apple pie spice

2   cups mashed banana

Add lime juice and spice to the mashed banana. Mix well. Do not warm sauce and use immediately. This fruity, thick sauce is good as a topping for frozen yogurt, sherbet, cakes, pancakes, and crêpes.

Variation: Substitute 2 cups persimmon for banana.

Teriyaki Turkey with Creamy Fruit Sauce   Yield: 4 servings

4   (4-ounce) turkey breast cutlets

1   cup prepared teriyaki sauce

1   cup mashed banana

1/2   cup avocado or moya purée

2   tablespoons Worcestershire sauce

Garnish: Fresh dill sprigs or 1 table-spoon dried dill

Marinate turkey in teriyaki sauce for at least 20 minutes. Remove turkey from marinade and boil marinade in small saucepan for 3 minutes. Coat grill rack with vegetable cooking spray. Place prepared grill rack over medium heat. Cook cutlets on rack 4 minutes on each side or until done. Baste turkey frequently with the marinade while cooking. Remove cutlets to a serving platter. Mix avocado purée and banana with Worcestershire sauce and cook over low heat to warm. Do not boil or overcook. Pour sauce over turkey and garnish with dill.

Alternate method: If unable to grill, lightly coat wok or skillet with vegetable cooking spray. Cook turkey cutlets 4 minutes on each side or until done. Proceed with directions.

Banana Daiquiri   Yield: 4 servings

For an exceptionally thick and icy cold daiquiri, freeze bananas before using.

3   medium bananas, sliced

8   ounces light rum

3   tablespoons lime juice

2   cups crushed ice

2   ounces brandy

Place all ingredients into a blender or food processor and use the knife blade to mix at high speed until foamy. Serve in iced, stemmed glasses.

Chocolate Fruitcake

Yield: 2 cakes

This recipe uses a combination of fresh fruit purée and dried fruit. The dried fruit is customarily available at health food, specialty, and nut and candy stores. If unavailable, dried apricots, dried dates, or dried figs can be substituted. Make cakes 2–3 weeks earlier than needed so flavors blend.

½	cup mashed banana or mashed persimmon
½	cup butter
½	cup brown sugar
3	egg whites
1	whole egg
1	teaspoon chocolate flavoring
½	cup guava purée or unsweetened applesauce, drained
½	cup pineapple purée, drained
¼	cup unsweetened cocoa
3½	cups all-purpose flour
¼	teaspoon baking soda
½	teaspoon salt
¼	teaspoon ground cloves
¼	teaspoon nutmeg
1½	teaspoons ground cinnamon
1½	teaspoons baking powder
¼	cup dried and diced papaya
¼	cup dried and diced pineapple
¼	cup dried and diced mango
¼	cup dried banana slices
½	cup currants
1	cup macadamia nut bits

Optional: Top with ½ cup flaked coconut; 6 tablespoons brandy or wine.

Cream together mashed banana, butter, and brown sugar. Add egg whites and egg, one at a time, beating after each addition. Blend in chocolate flavoring, guava purée, and pineapple purée. In another bowl, stir together cocoa, flour, baking soda, salt, spices, and baking powder. Add dried fruits and nuts. Stir the flour mixture into the creamed mixture until well blended. Line 5 by 9-inch loaf pans with heavy-duty foil to prevent over-browning during baking. Pour batter evenly into the pans. Top with coconut. Bake at 325° for 1¾ hours or until done. Cool completely in pans on a rack. Remove from pans, drizzle with brandy or wine to intensify flavors, wrap airtight or place in a wine-dampened cloth in a covered container, and store in the refrigerator. After cakes mellow, about 3 weeks, they can be frozen up to 6 months. To serve, cut cakes with a sharp, nonserrated knife or an electric knife.

Banana Carrot Cake

Yield: 1 cake

A sheet cake is easily prepared because it uses only one baking pan and can be frosted in the pan. It travels well and can be cut into squares and served from the baking pan. This recipe can also be made using a tube cake pan.

2	cups all-purpose flour
$1/2$	cup granulated sugar
$1/2$	cup brown sugar
$1/4$	teaspoon salt
2	teaspoons baking soda
$1/2$	teaspoon ground cloves
$1/2$	teaspoon ground allspice
1	cup mashed banana
$1/4$	cup vegetable oil
1	egg and 2 egg whites, slightly beaten
2	cups shredded carrots

Combine flour, sugars, salt, baking soda, cloves, and allspice in a large bowl. Stir in fruit. Add oil, eggs, and carrots. Stir and mix thoroughly. Coat 13 by 9 by 2-inch baking pan with vegetable cooking spray. Pour into prepared baking pan. Bake at 350° for 35–40 minutes or until toothpick inserted in center comes out clean. Cool in pan. Spread top with fruit frosting.

Fruit Frosting

1	(4-ounce) package of low-fat cream cheese, softened
$1/2$	cup mashed banana
2	teaspoons vanilla flavoring

Blend softened cream cheese, mashed banana, and vanilla flavoring. Spread on cooled cake.

Fast and Easy Banana Cake

Yield: 12 servings

Follow box directions for spice tube cake mix substituting 1 cup mashed banana for $1/4$ cup water. Bake in tube pan lightly coated with vegetable cooking spray.

Topping:

1	cup mashed bananas
1	carton banana or piña colada yogurt
1	tablespoon brown sugar

Mix all topping ingredients and drizzle over cool cake. Or warm topping and serve separately as a sauce for cake.

Chocolate-Chip Tropical Bread

Yield: 1 loaf

½ cup melted margarine

½ cup granulated sugar

½ cup brown sugar

2 eggs

1 cup mashed banana or mango

2 cups all-purpose flour

1 teaspoon baking powder

½ teaspoon baking soda

½ teaspoon salt

1 cup semisweet chocolate morsels

Optional: ½ cup macadamia nut bits.

Gradually add sugars to margarine in a medium-size bowl and beat at medium speed with electric mixer. Add eggs, one at a time, beating after each addition. Stir in fruit. Combine flour with baking powder and baking soda in a separate bowl. Gradually add to creamed mixture and blend. Be careful not to overmix the batter. Stir just to moisten the dry ingredients. The batter should not be smooth; lumps are fine. Stir in chips and nuts. Coat a 9 by 5 by 3-inch loaf pan lightly with vegetable cooking spray. Spoon batter into prepared pan. Bake at 350° for 70 minutes or until toothpick inserted into center comes out clean. A crack in the top of the loaf is typical. Cool in pan 10 minutes and remove from pan, cooling completely on a wire rack.

Banana Petits

Yield: 4 dozen

These miniature muffins are a perfect size for a coffee klatch or tea party.

½ cup whole-wheat flour

1 cup all-purpose flour

¼ cup crunchy cereal

⅓ cup sugar

2 teaspoons baking powder

1 tablespoon poppy seeds

¼ teaspoon salt

1 (8-ounce) carton banana or pineapple yogurt

¼ cup melted margarine

1 egg, beaten

1½ cups mashed banana

Combine first seven ingredients in a large bowl and stir. Combine yogurt, margarine, and eggs in a separate bowl. Blend and add to the dry ingredients. Stir to moisten. Gently fold in fruit. Lightly coat miniature muffin pans with vegetable cooking spray. Spoon batter into prepared muffin pans and fill to three-fourths full. Bake at 400° for 18 minutes or until done. Remove from pans immediately.

Frozen Bananas

It is possible to have over 100 bananas on a bunch ripening at once. Oftentimes, this is more than the average family can consume before the bananas spoil. Here are two ways to store bananas for later use. Select firm, straight bananas. Peel and skewer lengthwise with a wooden chopstick. Wrap securely and freeze. To serve, coat frozen banana with chocolate topping, which hardens on contact with a cold surface. Banana can be rolled in macadamia nut bits, crushed cereal, or wheat germ before chocolate hardens.

Select firm, ripe bananas and cut them into $1/2$-inch chunks. Pour enough pineapple or guava fruit juice over them to moisten. Dredge bananas in crushed chocolate cookie crumbs. Arrange banana chunks in a single layer on a baking sheet. Freeze until firm. Remove from sheet, wrap securely, and store up to 2 months.

Banana-Passion Fruit Sorbet   Yield: 6 servings

The passion fruit pulp gives a lovely texture and color to this sorbet. If it is unavailable, use crushed pineapple.

3   cups banana purée

$1/2$ cup passion fruit pulp with seeds or 1 (8-ounce) can crushed pineapple

1   tablespoon honey

Optional: Top each serving with 1 tablespoon dark rum.

Combine all ingredients and freeze until almost firm. Break mixture into large pieces and place into food processor bowl. Process with knife blade until fluffy but not thawed. Return to freezer and freeze until firm.

Breadfruit

Artocarpus altilis

*T*HERE IS A LEGEND that says that the early Polynesians carried breadfruit plants from Tahiti to Hawai'i centuries ago and supposedly planted them at Kualoa for an O'ahu chief. Breadfruit originated in Malaysia, probably New Guinea, and it has been eaten for more than 2,000 years. There are about 100 seedless varieties of breadfruit grown in Polynesia. It was first seen by Europeans at the Marquesas in 1595, and each successive Pacific voyage brought back information about breadfruit. Because the planters in the British West Indies wanted it as a cheap and nourishing food for their African laborers, they petitioned George III to bring breadfruit trees from Tahiti to the West Indies. The British Admiralty chose Lieutenant William Bligh, who had sailed with Captain James Cook on the *Resolution*, to command the *Bounty*.

Bligh sailed from England for Tahiti in December 1787. After 23 weeks of work, he left Tahiti with 1,015 breadfruit plants growing in tubs. In the succeeding mutiny, the precious breadfruit plants were thrown overboard. After his miraculous return to England, Bligh was given command of the *Providence* and instructed to go a second time to Tahiti for breadfruit. He sailed in August 1791 and gathered 2,125 breadfruit plants, which grew in pots on the quarterdeck. They were covered by canvas to protect them from salt air and were tended by two skilled botanists, James Wiles and Christopher Smith. This "floating garden" arrived in Jamaica in February 1793. Breadfruit is still grown extensively in the West Indies, Brazil, and most of Central America.

Although there are some seed-bearing breadfruit in Hawai'i, most island breadfruit is seedless. The traditional Hawaiian *'ulu* does not have seeds and is cultivated by root shoots. Some Polynesians used breadfruit as a staple in their diet, but the Hawaiians relied more on taro, sweet potatoes, and bananas. Research indicates that the Hawaiians brought with them only one kind of breadfruit, and this type is also found in the Marquesas Islands, Tahiti, and throughout Polynesia.

Hawaiians used the light wood of the breadfruit for drums, canoe hulls, and surfboards. The sap produced a gum used to fill canoe seams and to trap birds whose colorful feathers were made into capes and helmets. The breadfruit design, which incorporates the leaves and fruit, is used in contemporary quilts and jewelry.

The breadfruit, related to the fig and mulberry, is a tall, exquisite tree that can grow to sixty feet. Its foliage is luxuriant, with leathery, lobed leaves one to three feet long. The tree should bear fruit in 3–5 years if given good growing conditions, and will continue to bear for 30–40 years. The fruit is green, round, or oblong and about eight to ten inches in diameter with a thin, rough rind. The green rind turns to green-brown or yellow as the fruit matures.

Breadfruit is a collective fruit made from many tiny flowers growing together to make slightly fibrous flesh around the tough core. The flesh is white, bland, and starchy in the green stage, becoming light yellow and sweet in the ripe stage. It can weigh up to ten pounds, but usually weighs two to five pounds and ripens mostly during the summer months, with a small winter crop. Fruit is picked when the skin shows some milky sap but is still firm. Breadfruit should be picked before it softens on the tree. A tiny cut from the stalk end should expose creamy to yellow flesh for a ripe breadfruit.

Use

Breadfruit contains about the same amount of carbohydrates (sugar and starch) as taro or sweet potato, and the calcium content is higher than that of white potato. In a soup or stew, breadfruit resembles a potato although it has a firmer texture and is more flavorful. When the fruit is fully ripe, the starch changes to sugar. Breadfruit should be stored green because it ripens quickly. Refrigeration will slow down the ripening process, but it can only be kept a day or two once it is partially ripe. Ripe, uncooked breadfruit freezes well. Peel and core breadfruit and store chunks in freezer bags for up to 6 months.

Breadfruit is cooked by the same methods as white or sweet potatoes—boiled, steamed, baked, roasted, fried, mashed, creamed, puréed and used in soups, puddings, and cakes. Grate it for bread recipes and hash browns or cube it for salads and vegetable dishes. It is good cored, stuffed with meat or cheese, and baked. Roasting breadfruit in its peel in the microwave, the oven, or on the grill gives it a unique flavor. If using a sauce with breadfruit, be sure to use ample liquid because the breadfruit has enormous capacity to absorb.

A little oil can be rubbed onto hands and the knife to guard against breadfruit's sticky sap, or cut the fruit under water to help protect hands and knife. Quarter hard breadfruit for easier peeling. Remove the core, peel, and place the pieces in water to prevent discoloration. For softer fruit, score the peel and use a teaspoon to peel the ripe breadfruit skin. The core pulls out easily.

The ancient Hawaiians cooked their breadfruit whole in the *imu*, an underground oven. Today, breadfruit is cooked whole in the microwave or roasted in the oven. Although it can be peeled and cooked in water like a boiled potato, it is more flavorful cooked in the microwave or the oven. Choose a breadfruit that is a mature size, shows milky sap through the rind, and is firm. The flesh should be creamy to yellow.

Breadfruit Tips

✳ Mix cooked and mashed breadfruit with pineapple or banana chunks or purée it to resemble a sweet potato dish.

✳ Add peeled breadfruit chunks when cooking stew and soup. It retains its texture and is especially good because it absorbs the cooking juices.

✳ Mashed, ripe breadfruit added to a soup or stew gives flavor and a rich texture.

✳ Peel and core mature, firm breadfruit. Cut into chunks and place into microwave-safe container. Add ½ cup chopped onion and top breadfruit with 1 cup prepared process cheese sauce. Cover and cook at High 20 minutes or until tender.

✳ Remove the stem and core of a mature, firm breadfruit and fill the cavity with a rice and meat mixture or any mixture of vegetables including fresh spinach. Cook it according to microwave or oven roasting instructions.

✳ To microwave: Wash breadfruit and pierce the skin about 12 times in different places. Cook at High 20 minutes or until a skewer can pass easily through the rind. Cool. Cut in half and remove core and stem. Scoop out pulp or cut into wedges and peel. Season with margarine, salt, pepper, or whip breadfruit pulp with ¼ cup plain yogurt and ¼ cup sour cream.

✳ To oven roast: Wash and place whole breadfruit in a pan containing enough water to keep fruit from burning, about 1 inch. Cook at 350° for 1 hour or until a skewer can pass easily through the skin. Remove from oven, pull out core and stem, and cut breadfruit into halves. Follow serving suggestions in microwave preparation recipe.

Spanish Rice Breadfruit

Yield: 4 servings

1   breadfruit

¼   cup minced onion

½   cup cooked rice

½   cup cooked ground beef, chicken, or turkey

½   teaspoon Italian seasoning

¼   cup tomato sauce

Wash breadfruit. Remove stem and core. Combine remaining ingredients in a medium-size bowl. Stuff breadfruit with Spanish rice mixture. Cook breadfruit according to microwave or oven instructions. To serve stuffed breadfruit: Cool and peel the breadfruit. Cut it into wedges including the rice mixture.

Layered Breadfruit

Yield: 6 servings

1   cooked breadfruit, mashed or chunks

1   (14-ounce) package frozen and cooked squash

1   (9-ounce) package frozen French-style green beans

1   cup shredded onion

2   cups prepared spaghetti sauce

1   cup low-fat shredded Cheddar cheese

Lightly coat a 3-quart baking container with vegetable cooking spray. Layer all ingredients in prepared baking container beginning with breadfruit and ending with cheese. Cover and bake at 350° for 30 minutes.

Microwave method: Lightly coat microwave-safe container and layer all ingredients beginning with breadfruit and ending with cheese. Cover and cook at High 20 minutes. Let stand 5 minutes before serving.

Vegetable Stuffed Breadfruit

Yield: 4 servings

1   breadfruit
2   cups mixed vegetables or 3 cups fresh spinach
1/2   cup tomato sauce
Salt and pepper to taste

Wash breadfruit. Remove stem and core. Mix vegetables and tomato sauce. Stuff breadfruit with vegetable mixture. Cook breadfruit according to microwave or oven instructions.

To serve stuffed breadfruit: Cool and peel. Cut breadfruit into wedges including the vegetable mixture.

Breadfruit Salad

Yield: 4 servings

Breadfruit can be used instead of potato in salads. It is prepared with either a low-cholesterol mayonnaise or an oil and vinegar dressing.

3   cups diced firm, cooked breadfruit
1/4   cup wine vinegar
6   tablespoons olive oil
Salt and pepper to taste
1/4   cup minced green onion
1/2   cup tomato salsa
1/2   cup diced cucumber or celery
1   tablespoon celery seeds
1   cup shredded carrots
2   tablespoons minced parsley
1   tablespoon dill
2   tablespoons paprika
Optional: 1 tablespoon diced chilies, or to taste. Substitute 1/2 cup low-cholesterol mayonnaise for wine vinegar and olive oil.

Peel and core breadfruit and cut into wedges. Microwave to tender or cook to tender in boiling water and drain. For the dressing, whisk vinegar, olive oil, salt, and pepper in a small bowl. Place diced breadfruit in large bowl and toss it with half the dressing. Add remaining ingredients and dressing. Toss gently to blend. Cover and chill thoroughly until serving time. To serve, transfer salad to serving bowl and garnish with paprika.

Breadfruit Soup

Yield: 12 cups

2 cups thinly sliced leeks or onions

2 cups thinly sliced fresh mushrooms

1 ripe, firm breadfruit, peeled and diced

6 cups water

1 cup thinly sliced celery

2 cups shredded carrots

2 tablespoons chicken-flavored bouillon granules

1 tablespoon minced tarragon

2 tablespoons lime juice or passion fruit juice

1 teaspoon ground white pepper

Optional: 1 cup fresh asparagus tips, diced; or 2 cups tiny shrimp.

Lightly coat Dutch oven or large pan with vegetable cooking spray. Sauté leeks and mushrooms in prepared pan over medium heat. Add all remaining ingredients, except asparagus tips, to the leeks and mushrooms. Cover and simmer approximately 30 minutes or until breadfruit is tender. Transfer vegetable mixture in batches into container of an electric blender or food processor and process until smooth. Return vegetable purée to the pan, add asparagus tips or tiny shrimp, and heat to warm. Ladle soup into individual bowls.

South Seas Brochette

Yield: 6 servings

6   (12-inch) skewers

2   pounds boneless lamb, chicken, or turkey, cut into 1½-inch cubes

Marinade:

¼   cup concentrated guava juice or other fruit juice

2   passion fruit, pulp and seeds or ¼ cup fruit purée

2   tablespoons olive oil

½   cup low-sodium soy sauce

2   tablespoons dark rum, red wine, or brown sugar

1   unpeeled and minced lime

2   teaspoons caraway seeds

1   tablespoon coarse black pepper

1   tablespoon fresh rosemary

Brochette:

½   mature, firm breadfruit or 2 cups potato chunks, partially cooked

1   sweet red pepper

12   whole fresh mushrooms

1   cup fresh pineapple chunks

Optional: 2 cups coarsely chopped watercress.

Trim fat from meat and place cubes into a shallow pan. Mix the marinade ingredients in a small bowl and pour over meat. Refrigerate at least 8 hours, turning cubes occasionally. Remove meat from marinade and pour marinade into a saucepan. Place marinade over medium heat, bring to a boil, and simmer 2 minutes.

Wash and pierce breadfruit. Microwave at High until tender, approximately 15 minutes. When cool, peel and core breadfruit and cut it into 2-inch pieces. Stove-top method: Peel, core, and cut breadfruit into wedges. Parboil breadfruit over medium heat to firm but tender. Cool and cut into 2-inch pieces. Cut red pepper into strips that can be wrapped around the breadfruit chunks. Thread skewers, alternating all ingredients. Grill over medium hot coals 8 minutes or to taste, turning and basting occasionally. Arrange watercress on a serving platter. Place skewers on watercress and serve the remaining marinade separately after heating it to boiling.

Marinade food safety: Marinades can be a breeding ground for bacteria. They contain all the dangers of raw meat. Marinade mixture should be boiled after the meat is removed and before using it for basting. If marinade is used toward the end of cooking, allow sufficient cooking time to kill any bacteria.

Carambola

Averrhoa carambola

*T*HE CARAMBOLA TREE has delicate, light green foliage; small pink flowers; and an abundance of golden-yellow fruits. It is about twenty feet tall and begins to bear fruit in the third year. Normally, there are two or three crops a year, and its season in Hawai'i is usually May–June and again in November–December, making it possible to have fruit intermittently from May through December.

The fruit is named for Averrhoës, a twelfth-century Arabic physician and philosopher. Carambola is the Portuguese name for the fruit. The Sanskrit name, *karmara*, meaning appetizer, is appropriate because the fresh, crisp, juicy fruit enhances any first course.

The carambola, also called star fruit and five corners, is native to India, China, and Indonesia. When it was introduced into Hawai'i is not known, but it could have come with the sandalwood traders. The fruit is grown commercially in Florida, New Zealand, Thailand, Africa, Israel, and Central and South America as well as Hawai'i. It is appearing more frequently in the marketplace and on restaurant menus. The oval fruits are greenish yellow and deepen to yellow-gold when ripe. They are three to seven inches long and four to eleven inches in diameter with five clearly defined, lengthwise ridges. The thin skin is edible, and the translucent flesh is juicy, fragrant, and pleasant. Carambola comes in many varieties, but can be divided into sweet or tart types.

Use

Select star fruits that have no brown spots. If the ribs show a brown line, remove them. This increases the sweet fruit flavor because it eliminates the oxalic acid in the ribs. The fruit does not discolor when sliced and adds crunch and texture when combined with softer tropical fruits in a salad, salsa, or sauce.

Unripe and firm, the fruit is used as a souring agent like tamarind and can replace lime and lemon slices in food or drinks. Ripe caram-bola makes an unusual garnish for punch, beverages, fruit salads, cakes, cheesecake, and pies. The pulp can be puréed and frozen. Use it in sauces for meat, fish, and poultry; in salad dressing; and in fruit vinegar. It makes wonderful relishes, chutney, and pickles. Although both sweet and tart types are suitable for these recipes, the sweet type is preferred for snacks.

To make carambola stars: Trim $1/8$ inch from the carambola ribs. Slice crosswise in $1/4$-inch slices to form stars.

❊❊❊❊❊❊❊

Star Fruit Salsa

Yield: 3 cups

2   cups thinly sliced star fruit

1   ($2^1/4$-ounce) can sliced ripe olives

$1/2$ cup diced sweet, red pepper

2   tablespoons olive oil

$1/2$ cup red wine or $1/4$ cup vinegar

1   cup diced red or green onion

1   tablespoon minced gingerroot

1   teaspoon black pepper

2   tiny red chili peppers, minced, or
     $3/4$ teaspoon minced jalapeño

2   tablespoons minced Chinese
     parsley (cilantro) or 2 tablespoons
     minced mint or basil

Combine all ingredients.

Serve with poultry, seafood, ham, beef, lamb, and Mexican food. Flavors blend if refrigerated at least 2 hours or overnight. This salsa becomes a dip with the addition of 1 (8-ounce) carton plain yogurt.

Spicy Star Fruit Dip

Yield: 5 cups

1 (8-ounce) carton papaya yogurt or lemon yogurt

1 cup chili sauce

1/2 cup diced celery

1 tablespoon minced chives

1 cup imitation crab or 1 (4¼-ounce) can shrimp, drained and finely chopped

2 cups minced carambola

2 tablespoons Worcestershire sauce

Optional: Bottled chili pepper sauce to taste.

Combine all ingredients. If a smooth dip is preferred, place all ingredients in food processor bowl. Process with metal blade to desired consistency. Cover and chill at least 1 hour. This dip also makes an unusual stuffing for baked potatoes or a colorful sauce for breadfruit.

Star Fruit Chutney

Yield: approximately 6 pints

3 cups cider vinegar

1½ cups dark brown sugar

10 cups star fruit slices (about 12 carambola) cut ¼ inch crosswise

3 cups shredded carrots

1 cup golden raisins

1 tablespoon pickling spice

1 tablespoon red pepper flakes

1 tablespoon ground cardamom

2 tablespoons lime zest

¼ cup finely chopped fresh ginger-root

Place vinegar and brown sugar in a large pan over medium heat and stir to dissolve. Add remaining ingredients. Simmer and stir constantly to mix well. The chutney can be cooked to desired consistency over low heat or finished in the microwave.

Microwave method: Place 4 cups of the chutney mixture into a 2-quart pourable glass measure. Microwave at High to desired consistency, stirring every 3 minutes. Pour or spoon into sterilized jars or freezer bags. Repeat procedure for remaining ingredients. Refrigerate the chutney up to 1 month or freeze up to 3 months.

Spicy Sausage with Carambola Chutney   Yield: 12 servings

1   pound spicy sausage, cooked and
    cut in 1-inch cubes

1   cup white wine

2   tablespoons prepared mustard

1/2 cup carambola or pineapple
    chutney

Cocktail picks

Microwave wine, mustard, and chutney in medium microwave-safe bowl at High 3 minutes. Add cooked and cubed sausage. Microwave at High 3 minutes. Stove-top method: Cook wine, mustard, and chutney over medium heat for 2 minutes. Add cooked and cubed sausage and continue to cook on low for 3 minutes. Remove sausage and sauce to a serving dish and provide cocktail picks.

Chicken Teri-Fruit Kabobs   Yield: 4 servings

1   cup low-sodium soy sauce

1/4 cup whiskey or fruit juice

1   tablespoon shredded gingerroot
    or gingerroot juice

1   crushed garlic clove

3   cups chicken chunks cut into
    1-inch cubes

1   cup carambola stars or lychee
    halves

1   cup pummelo or firm papaya
    chunks, cut into 1-inch cubes

3   tablespoons olive oil

3   tablespoons passion fruit juice or
    orange juice

1   teaspoon tarragon leaves

Combine soy sauce, whiskey, gingerroot, and garlic. Mix well and add chicken chunks. Refrigerate and marinate at least 2 hours. Drain chicken and discard marinade. Thread chicken onto wooden skewers. Thread fruit onto separate skewers. Combine olive oil, fruit juice, and tarragon. Baste fruit kabobs. Place chicken kabobs on a microwave-safe roasting rack or in a shallow, microwave-safe baking dish. Baste with flavored oil. Cover with waxed paper and microwave at High for 6–8 minutes, rearranging kabobs and basting every 2 minutes. Warm fruit kabobs the last 2 minutes. Alternate method: Broil chicken kabobs in oven 5 inches from heat for 3–4 minutes, turning and basting until done. Broil fruit the last 2 minutes to warm. Cool slightly and reassemble kabobs, alternating chicken and fruit on fresh skewers before serving. Refrigerate if not using promptly. These kabobs are good cold or at room temperature. Although it may take more time to prepare and cook the fruit and the chicken on separate skewers, it is worth it. The fruit comes out firm, yet warm, and not overcooked.

Star Fruit Relish

Yield: 2 cups

2   cups minced carambola

1   (4-ounce) can chopped green chilies, drained

1/2   cup diced green onion

4   tablespoons diced pimiento

1/4   cup macadamia nut pieces, walnut bits, or currants

1/4   cup vinegar

Bottled chili pepper sauce to taste

Combine all ingredients and chill overnight to blend flavors. Relish can be refrigerated for 2 weeks. This hot relish is good with cream cheese as an appetizer or on ham and rye sandwiches.

Carambola-Broccoli Salad

Yield: 8 servings

4   cups broccoli flowerets

1   cup carambola stars

1/2   cup golden raisins

1/2   cup red onion rings

1/4   cup sliced water chestnuts

1/4   cup plain yogurt

1/4   cup low-cholesterol mayonnaise

Combine the first five ingredients and toss gently. Blend the yogurt and mayonnaise in a small bowl and stir the salad dressing into broccoli mixture. Cover and chill thoroughly before serving.

Star Fruit Vinegar

Yield: 4 cups

4 cups vinegar

1/4 cup honey

3 cups diced and unpeeled star fruit or guava

Optional: 2 leafy sprigs of mint.

Use a nonaluminum pan to bring vinegar and honey almost to a boil over medium heat. Place fruit and mint into the container and cover tightly. Let stand covered at room temperature 48 hours. Strain vinegar and discard fruit and mint. Refrigerate vinegar up to 6 months. Use this tangy vinegar when making salad dressings, tart sauces, and marinades.

Pink Star Fruit Breakfast Spread

Yield: 4 cups

1 1/2 cups carambola half stars

1 1/2 cups lychee quarters

1/4 cup guava juice

1 teaspoon almond flavoring

1 teaspoon ground coriander

1 teaspoon ground nutmeg

1 package fruit pectin for light jam

Optional: 2 tablespoons honey or to taste.

Place all ingredients except honey in a 3- to 4-quart saucepan over medium heat. Stir to dissolve pectin and bring to a rapid boil. Boil 1 minute, stirring constantly. Remove from heat. Honey can be stirred into the spread before freezing or before it is served. Pour into sterilized containers or freezer bags. Cool at room temperature 24 hours and then freeze up to 6 months or refrigerate for 3 months. Do not store at room temperature.

Sweet-Sour Star Fish

Yield: 2 servings

Lemon juice, lemon grass, and star fruit complement and blend to give an exotic flavor to island fish. This do-ahead dish provides ease of preparation at mealtime.

1	pound mahimahi, ono, swordfish, or sole fillets
3	tablespoons lemon juice
1	tablespoon brown sugar
1	medium onion, chopped
2	garlic cloves
1/2	inch gingerroot
1/4	teaspoon turmeric
1/4	cup macadamia nut bits
1	stalk lemon grass, bruised
4	tablespoons water
2	carambolas, thinly sliced

Marinate fish in lemon juice and brown sugar mixture. Refrigerate for at least 1 hour. Purée the next five ingredients to a smooth paste. Place a heavy pan or wok over medium heat. Add purée, lemon grass, and water. Simmer 2 minutes; add carambola, fish fillets, and marinade. Cook to tender, about 10 minutes. Cool. Remove fish and sauce to a suitable container, cover, and refrigerate overnight, if possible, to intensify flavors. If time does not permit, cool fish at least 2 hours. To serve, reheat in a microwave-safe container at Medium High for 3 minutes or reheat in the oven at 300° for 5 minutes. Do not overcook fish.

Carambola and Caraway Noodles
Yield: 4 servings

1	(8-ounce) package noodles
1/4	cup macadamia nut or olive oil
1/2	cup minced carambola
1	tablespoon caraway seeds

Cook noodles according to package directions; drain well. Warm oil in a small skillet over low heat and add remaining ingredients. Stir and mix for 30 seconds; do not cook. Place noodles on a warmed serving platter and drizzle with the carambola-caraway mixture. Toss until noodles are well coated.

Star Shrimp

This simple dish is fast and easy to prepare. The addition of tropical fruit makes an ordinary shrimp sauté more unusual, flavorful, and attractive.

1   pound shrimp, shelled and cleaned

2   carambolas, 2 passion fruit, or 1 cup fresh or canned lychee halves (if combining fruit, amount should equal 1 cup)

2   tablespoons olive oil

1/2 teaspoon ground cardamom

1   tablespoon sesame seeds

Coarsely ground black pepper to taste

3   tablespoons dry vermouth or gin

Trim 1/8 inch from star fruit ribs and slice crosswise into 1/4-inch stars. If using passion fruit, cut crosswise and scoop out and use both pulp and seeds. If using canned lychees, drain and halve them, saving the juice for another use. Heat olive oil in wok or skillet over medium heat. Add cardamom and sesame seeds and cook 15 seconds to release flavors. Do not burn. Add shrimp and fruit. Sauté 2 minutes or until shrimp turns pink. Do not overcook. Toss shrimp and fruit with coarse black pepper and vermouth. Serve immediately.

Star Fruit Wine Sorbet

1   envelope unflavored gelatin.

1/4 cup pomegranate pulp including seeds or 1/4 cup cranberry juice

1   cup plum wine

2   tablespoons honey

2   cups carambola purée

1/2 cup minced fresh mint

Garnish: 4 tablespoons crystallized ginger

In a small saucepan, sprinkle gelatin over pomegranate pulp, wine, and honey. Let stand 5 minutes. Cook over low heat and stir constantly to dissolve gelatin and honey. Cool. Add the carambola purée and minced mint. Stir. Cover and freeze until firm. Position knife blade in food processor bowl and add frozen mixture. Process until smooth, but do not completely thaw. Scoop sorbet into individual dessert dishes and return to freezer to harden. Garnish with crystallized ginger before serving. Serve this glittery, elegant dessert with a crisp wafer cookie.

Star Fruit Pickles

Yield: 3 quarts

24 star fruit cut into 1/2-inch stars

2 onions

2 sweet red or green peppers

3 large carrots

3 celery stalks

7 cups water

2 cups white vinegar

4 tablespoons salt

3 garlic cloves, quartered and crushed

3 tiny red chili peppers, deseeded and halved

3 teaspoons pickling spice

Place carambola stars in large bowl. Cut onions and the sweet peppers into 1-inch pieces and add to carambola. Cut carrots and celery into 2-inch lengths and add to mixture. Toss. Heat water, vinegar, and salt to boiling. Keep hot while dividing the star mixture among sterilized jars. To each jar, add four garlic pieces, two pieces of chili pepper, and 1 teaspoon pickling spice. Pour hot liquid into sterilized jars and fill to 1/8 inch of rim. Close jars and cool the pickles. Refrigerate and use within 6 months.

Citrus

ALL CITRUS ORIGINATED in China or Southeast Asia. Citrus is documented in ancient Sanskrit, where the word *naranga* is used for orange and *vijapura* for lemon. Early cultivators reduced the seediness and improved the size and juiciness of wild citrus. They transported it to Mesopotamia and from there it was carried throughout the world. The Arabs spread citrus not only to Africa but also to Spain and Portugal, where the fruit was widely cultivated. Columbus took oranges and lemons with him to begin crops in the New World.

This early cultivation of the fruit resulted in many types and hybrids of citrus, which even today are continually expanding. Most citrus are evergreen with shiny, light to dark green leaves and white, very fragrant flowers. Their skin is oily, bitter, and orange-yellow to bright green. Because Hawaiian citrus is not treated with gas or subjected to cold weather, it does not usually produce the bright orange skin color found on mainland fruits. The nutritious citrus flesh or juice not only intensifies the flavors of foods, marinades, and sauces, but also adds vitamins and minerals.

Calamondin   *Citrus mitis*

This small, spiny, shrublike citrus tree is native to the Philippines. Scientists suspect it is a cross between the kumquat and the mandarin. It is a heavy bearer of one-inch bright, tangerine-shaped fruits. Both the skin and flesh can be eaten although the fruit is very sour, similar to a lemon. The fruit has a thin skin that peels easily, few seeds, and six to ten segments.

Use

Calamondin can be substituted for lemon in most recipes. Use it for marmalades, sauces, marinades, and beverages. Serve it with papaya and melons to enhance their flavor.

Grapefruit   *Citrus maxima*

The first description of grapefruit came from Barbados in 1750, where a cross between pummelo (shaddock) and orange may have occurred naturally. The name "grapefruit" was used in Jamaica early in the nineteenth century because the fruit grew in clusters like grapes. Grapefruit was recognized as a species in 1830 and grown commercially in Florida about 1880.

The term *pomelo* is sometimes used for grapefruit, but should not be confused with pummelo, which, although somewhat similar to the grapefruit, has many different characteristics. The grapefruit is a smaller fruit, grows in clusters, and has few seeds, a thinner skin, and juicier flesh than the pummelo.

Grapefruit trees grow to twenty to forty feet and are larger than orange trees. The fruits are round, four to six inches in diameter, with yellow-green skin that can be thin or very thick. The flesh, mildly acid to very acid, is yellow, pink-yellow, or reddish and has segments separated by a membrane. The juiciness and sweetness of the flesh depend on the variety and on growing conditions.

Grapefruit was introduced into Hawai'i at an early, unknown date and was documented in the Islands by Hillebrand before 1871. The grapefruit grown in Hawai'i are of excellent quality.

Use

Grapefruit is a good appetite stimulant. The Chinese serve it as an appetizer and this has been copied in America, where half a grapefruit is served for breakfast or grapefruit segments are included in a fruit cocktail. Grapefruit can be sweetened with white or brown sugar, honey, or sherry.

Grapefruit combines well in vegetable, fruit, and seafood salads. It mixes with bland tropical fruits or salad greens and is good with soft cheeses or made into jellies, marmalade, and candied peel. The segments or cut rounds can be used with poultry, seafood, beef, and ham. Canned grapefruit sections can be used in salads or entrées. As with all citrus, the heavier the fruit, the greater the juice yield. If fruit is left unchilled, the juice yield is lower.

Lemon   *Citrus limon*

The origin of the lemon is India, Burma, and southern China. It still grows wild in the Himalaya Mountains, and pips from lemons or limes, estimated to be 4,000 years old, have been found in West Asia. Murals at Pompeii depicted lemons, but they became popular in Europe after the Crusades.

The lemon tree is medium-sized, less than twenty feet. The fruit size varies from small to as large as an orange, and the fruit shape is oval to round. The greenish yellow or orange skin can be thin and smooth or thick and coarse. The strongest lemon flavor comes from the fragrant skin, which contains an essential oil of lemon and is used as "zest." To obtain this, grate the skin, avoiding the white pith. The fruit has eight to ten segments, and the flesh is juicy and sour. Lemons will ripen off the tree if picked green, although the flavor improves if the fruit ripens on the tree.

Lemon plants were introduced into Hawai'i early in the nineteenth century. The Hawaiians called the rough lemon (*Citrus limonia*) *kukane*, the names of two Hawaiian gods. They liked the lemon for its fragrant skin, but did not eat the sour pulp. Although lemon trees bear most of the year in Hawai'i, there is usually a period of 1 or 2 months in the spring when lemons are not produced.

Use

Lemons and limes, sprinkled with water and refrigerated in plastic bags, last a month or more. Frozen, the juice and zest (grated peel) last 4 months. The average juice yield per lemon is 3–5 tablespoons, but to extract more juice, microwave the lemon at 50 percent power 1½ minutes. It takes five to six lemons for a cup of juice. A medium lemon yields 3 teaspoons of zest.

Citric acid preserves natural color in the flesh of certain fruits that turn brown when exposed to air. Squeeze a little lemon juice over apples, bananas, and avocados to keep their fresh appearance. Substitute lemon juice for vinegar in salad dressings or mayonnaise, and use it in marinades and sauces to tenderize meat. Grate the peel for use in desserts, salads, vegetables, jams, sorbet, and frostings. Remove fish, garlic, and onion odors from hands with lemon juice. Fresh lemon is a colorful garnish, and it also makes wonderful lemonade as well as blending with other fruit juices.

Lime   *Citrus aurantifolia*

The lime tree is a small, bushy evergreen that grows to a height of eighteen to twenty feet. It can also be shaped to form a hedge. Its origin, the same as the lemon, is in India, Burma, and southern China. In Egypt, the lime was more common than the lemon. In late eighteenth-century

England, limes were issued to British sailors with their rum ration to prevent scurvy, and they became known as "limeys."

Limes are round or oval and about one and a half to two and a half inches in diameter. Although limes are customarily picked green, ripe limes may be green or yellow, but should be firm. The lime's thin skin is fragrant and is used in making perfumes. The flesh is yellow-green to green, juicy, and pleasantly tart. The average lime, half the size of a lemon, contains one-third more citric acid. The Bearss variety, also called Persian or Tahitian, is medium-sized with a fragrant rind that gives an exotic flavor to foods. The Chinese and Mexican varieties are called Key Limes. A lime hybrid, the limequat, is a result of crossing the lime and the kumquat.

The lime, requiring a frost-free location, is cultivated mainly in the tropics. It seems the most adaptable of the citrus fruits to Hawai'i, where limes are nearly always in season. The heaviest crop comes in late summer and fall.

Use

Limes can be refrigerated for at least a month, and both juice and zest freeze well. The citrus flavor enhances fish, meat, and poultry dishes as well as fruit salads and desserts. Fanciful lime segments or slices make a colorful garnish. Lime juice can be substituted for lemon juice, but only half the amount is needed because lime juice is more potent. An average lime yields 2–3 tablespoons of juice. Lime juice makes a good marinade for chicken or veal and is used with raw fish, Tahitian style. The fruit can be used in jams, jellies, marmalades, and spicy pickles. Lime is excellent for sorbet, cake fillings, and pies. The juice is good in punches, cocktails, and beverages. Use it in soups with a ratio of 1 tablespoon lime juice to 3 cups of soup.

Orange   *Citrus sinensis*

The orange, most popular of the citrus group, is native to China and Southeast Asia. It was widely spread throughout the Arab Empire, into Europe, and, especially, into the Mediterranean countries. It is possible that the golden apples described in Greek mythology were oranges. Spanish ships in the fourteenth century brought the first oranges to England, where they became popular with royalty. Much later, in 1805, orange orchards were started in California, followed quickly by orchards in Florida.

There are many varieties of oranges. The sweet orange, known in Hawai'i as " Kona orange," is a Valencia introduced into the Islands in 1792. Archibald Menzies, surgeon and naturalist aboard *Discovery*, grew orange plants on shipboard from seeds taken at the Cape of Good Hope. He distributed them to Hawaiian chiefs. A year later, Menzies returned to Kona and saw a dozen orange trees described in his journal as "growing luxuriantly." In Kailua-Kona, some of the original root stock still bears heavily. The Kona orange should not be confused with the navel (seedless) orange being grown in Ka'ū. The sweet orange is tight skinned, round, about three inches in diameter, with a solid core and juicy, sweet pulp divided into ten to thirteen segments. The customary eating oranges, Valencia and navel, are also called sweet orange. In Hawai'ı, there are three times more Valencias planted than navels. Other varieties of sweet oranges include Spanish (large and coarse grained), Mediterranean (fine grained), and blood orange (red flesh with a unique hint of raspberries).

The bitter orange *(Citrus aurantium)*, sometimes called Seville or sour orange, is similar to the sweet orange, but has a thick rind, many seeds, and pulp that is not eaten raw. It is made into marmalades or grown for its scented flowers and oils used in making perfumes. The highly aromatic rind is utilized in bitters.

Use

To peel and section an orange family style: Use the tip of a knife to cut through the peel but not into the fruit. Make a lengthwise cut around the circumference of the orange, dividing it in half. Then make another lengthwise cut around the circumference of the orange, dividing it into quarters. Peel the orange from top to bottom. This technique can also be used on grapefruit, dividing the larger fruit into eight pieces before peeling.

Orange is a versatile fruit, blending with many other fruits and needing no sweetening. An orange sauce complements poultry, ham, and fish, and the juice sweetens marinades, grilled potatoes, breads, cake batters, and frostings. The peel is good in preserves and chutney.

Pummelo   *Citrus maxima*

Pummelo, also called shaddock and Chinese grapefruit, is native to Malaysia and spread north into China. It is named for Captain Shaddock, commander of an East India Company ship, who took the first pummelo seeds to Jamaica in 1696. The pummelo should not be confused with pomelo, another name for grapefruit. It does not grow in clusters and differs from the grapefruit in size, shape, texture, and, most of all, flavor. The pummelo is highly prized in Southeast Asia, where it is judged the best of all citrus fruits for desserts and other culinary purposes. Pummelo develops its superior quality in warm, tropical areas, where it grows best in sheltered areas near sea level. It tolerates brackish water and poor drainage. It is grown commercially in China, Thailand, Malaysia, Indonesia, Taiwan, the Philippines, and Vietnam, and throughout the world in tropical areas by backyard gardeners.

The pummelo reaches fifteen to thirty feet in height and has three- to eight-inch leaves. The round or pear-shaped fruit, the largest of any citrus species, tapers at the stem end and has many seeds. The diameter is five to ten inches, and although it can weigh up to fifteen pounds, two to three pounds is normal. Size varies from that of a baby cantaloupe to nearly a basketball. The thick skin is greenish yellow, and when it is removed, the fruit may be smaller than a grapefruit.

The pummelo flesh, consisting of eleven to fourteen segments, is pleasantly dry, sweet, and slightly pink. Color, juiciness, and sweetness of the fruit depend on variety and on growing conditions. Because the sweet pummelo lacks the astringency of grapefruit and usually has a drier pulp, it is ideally suited to many recipes. To obtain maximum sweetness, ripen pummelo off the tree at room temperature for 10–15 days. In Thailand, pummelo is picked when it loses its dark green color, and then it is stored indoors for 1 or 2 months to improve flavor and juiciness. Determine the ripeness of pummelo by its heavy aroma and deepening yellow color.

Use

Select a heavy fruit, test for ripeness by its fragrance, and if there is a strong, sweet aroma, refrigerate. Pummelo keeps at least a month under refrigeration.

A half fruit is not usually served because of the size and the toughness of the segment membranes. Remove all heavy pith and membrane for use in vegetable or fruit salads, desserts, and entrées. It can be puréed and used for jams, sauces, marinades, and ices. The rind can be preserved or used in marmalade.

Mandarin Orange/Tangerine *Citrus reticulata*

The tangerine is probably the best known and most extensively planted of the mandarin orange varieties, which include king orange, temple orange, tangelo (a cross between mandarin and grapefruit), tangor (a cross between mandarin and sweet orange), and the Satsuma mandarin (*Citrus unshiu*), the principal variety in Japan and central China, although it does not bear well in Hawai'i. Mandarin is used for all members of this type of citrus fruit. Leaves of a true mandarin are called "seed leaves" and are a pistachio-green color.

The mandarin orange can be traced back to Cochin China, former name for the southernmost region of Vietnam. It first appeared in Europe and the United States in the nineteenth century, although it has been cultivated in Japan for 2,000 years. Mandarin takes its name from a group of high-ranking public officials in imperial China whose hats had a button shaped similarly to the fruit and whose robes were the color of the fruit.

The tangerine tree is smaller than the orange tree but is more resistant to cold. The fruit is two to three inches in diameter, round, and flat on top and bottom. The rough, loose, highly aromatic skin can be brilliant red-orange. However, those grown in Hawai'i sometimes have a greenish hue. The color of the skin does not indicate sweetness. The fruit is easily peeled and reveals a deep-orange, juicy, sweet flesh having ten segments and numerous seeds.

Tangerines grow throughout Hawai'i from sea level to 2,000 feet, doing particularly well in the cooler valleys. Fruits are normally available October through January.

The Satsuma tree, named for a former feudal province of southern Kyushu, Japan, has larger, broader leaves and bears fruit similar to the tangerine but with few seeds. This tree is said to have come from Eternal Land at the request of the Mikado. In Japan, the song of the cuckoo and the fragrance of the fruit are poetically associated.

Use

Select heavy fruits that are not shriveled. Tangerine juice can replace orange juice in recipes. One-third of the fruit crop in America is used for juice, sherbet, and canned sections, and two-thirds is used as fresh fruit. Segments are wonderful in spinach salad, rice or stuffing, fruit salad, sauce, and sorbet and with vegetables and entrées. The grated peel is good in puddings, fillings, and frostings and can be made into marmalade. Store in the refrigerator for up to 2 weeks.

Kumquat   *Fortunella margarita*

The kumquat was named for Robert Fortunel, who introduced the fruit into Europe in 1846. It is a native of China, where it is called *chin chu*

(Mandarin) or *kam kwat* (Cantonese), meaning golden orange. Kumquat has been cultivated for thousands of years in China and Japan.

The kumquat tree is small, rarely exceeding ten feet, and is sometimes grown in a container as an ornamental or grown as a hedge. In Hawai'i the tree blossoms and fruits continually. It is hardier than other citrus and can be grown in colder climates. Fruit ripens slowly on the tree and changes from green to brilliant orange. It is the size of a giant olive, about one inch, oval, with a smooth skin. Both skin and flesh are edible, but the tart flesh overpowers the more delicate flavor of the peel. The tiny seeds in the four to six segments are not objectionable.

Kumquats were among the early fruits introduced into Hawai'i and were named by Hillebrand in 1888 as growing wild along with other citrus. This prolific evergreen shrub is found in home gardens but is not grown commercially in Hawai'i as it is in Florida and California. The kumquat has been crossed to produce the limequat and the orangequat.

Use

Select firm, orange fruits. The most common use for kumquat is decorating the ends of a crown roast of lamb. They can be minced and used with poultry, ham salads, muffins and breads, salad dressings, sorbet, cakes, and frostings. They are good preserved, substituted in beverages for limes and lemons, and made into jams and marmalade. They make a colorful sauce and a beautiful garnish. Kumquats will keep 1 month if refrigerated.

Pummelo and Pomegranate Appetizer

Yield: 8 servings

This is a simple yet excellent first course for a sit-down dinner party. Pummelo is an appetite stimulant, and its natural sweetness should not be destroyed with a sugar addition; but its dryness can be supplemented with a liquid to intensify the pummelo's flavor.

1   pummelo

1   pomegranate

1/2   cup dry sherry or red wine

Garnish: 8 fresh mint sprigs

Peel and remove membranes from pummelo segments. Cut segments into bite-size pieces. Peel pomegranate and remove the red, juicy seeds from the white pith. Combine the fruits and the dry sherry, cover, and refrigerate overnight or at least 6 hours. Select appropriate appetizer plates that will show off the jewel tones of the fruits. Divide the appetizer among the plates and garnish with fresh mint sprigs.

Three-Fruit Salad

Yield: 4 servings

This delicious salad is convincing evidence that the tomato can be used successfully as a fruit. Dice all fruit into 1/2 to 3/4-inch pieces. Do not make large chunks.

2   cups diced pummelo (if pummelo is unavailable, use orange or grapefruit)

2   cups diced tomato

2   cups diced firm banana

1   cup finely diced onion

Dressing:

1/4   cup guava–passion fruit concentrated juice or other fruit juice

1/2   cup plain yogurt

1   tablespoon curry powder

1/4   teaspoon black pepper

Mānoa, butter, or red lettuce leaves to line salad bowl

Mix all fruits and onion in a medium-sized bowl. Blend dressing ingredients thoroughly in small bowl and pour over salad ingredients. Toss gently. Line a serving bowl with lettuce, add salad, and serve chilled.

Tropical Citrus Salad Bowl

Yield: 8 servings

1   bunch watercress, washed, dried, and coarsely chopped

1   bunch spinach, washed, dried, and coarsely chopped

1   bunch romaine lettuce, washed, dried, and coarsely chopped

5   cups diced citrus segments (choose from grapefruit, orange, pummelo, tangerine)

1/2 cup sliced ripe olives

1   jícama, peeled and thinly sliced

Dressing:

1/2 cup pineapple juice or orange juice

1   garlic clove, crushed

3   tablespoons macadamia oil or olive oil

1/2 teaspoon cumin

1/2 teaspoon coriander seeds

1/2 teaspoon dry mustard

1   tablespoon lime or lemon zest

Combine all salad ingredients in salad bowl. Thoroughly blend dressing ingredients and pour over salad. Toss before serving.

Kumquat Sauce

Yield: 1½ cups

1   cup minced kumquat
1   teaspoon curry powder
½   teaspoon oregano
1   teaspoon ginger powder
½   teaspoon thyme
1   garlic clove, crushed
½   cup white wine
2   teaspoons macadamia oil or
     olive oil
1   tablespoon pineapple, papaya, or
     mango fruit spread
Optional: 2 tablespoons currants or
     golden raisins.

Warm all ingredients over low heat to mix thoroughly. Do not boil.

Microwave method: Place all ingredients into a 2-quart pourable glass measure. Stir to mix. Cook at High 2 minutes. This sauce is good on fish or poultry.

Fast Grapefruit Sauce

Yield: 2 cups

1   tablespoon grapefruit zest
1   cup fresh grapefruit juice
Sections from 1 grapefruit, coarsely
     chopped
3   tablespoons red wine
2   tablespoons spicy mustard
1   teaspoon honey

Thoroughly mix all ingredients. Sauce can be used for roasting in the oven or cooking in the microwave. Serve with ham or poultry. Remove meat when cooking is finished. Defat and reduce sauce.

Citrus Fruit Vinegar

Yield: 4 cups

A fruit vinegar is good in salad dressing, sauce, and marinade. Lemon, lime, orange, pummelo, and kumquat make excellent vinegar.

4 cups vinegar

¼ cup honey

3 cups diced, unpeeled citrus

Use a nonaluminum pan to bring vinegar and honey almost to a boil over medium heat. Stir fruit into the container and cover tightly. Let stand covered at room temperature for 48 hours. Strain vinegar and discard fruit. Refrigerate vinegar up to 6 months.

Kumquat Wine Relish

Yield: 8 servings

½ cup minced fresh kumquat

1 (12-ounce) package fresh cranberries

3 tablespoons honey

½ cup red wine

1 cinnamon stick

½ teaspoon mace

Wash and drain cranberries. Combine and mix all ingredients in 3-quart microwave-safe bowl. Cover loosely and microwave at High for 10 minutes until berries burst. Discard cinnamon stick. Cover and chill before serving. Can store in refrigerator up to 1 month. Serve this tart and colorful relish with turkey or pork.

Grilled Hawaiian Fish

Yield: 4 servings

The delicate flavor of the fish can be varied by the choice of tropical fruit. This recipe is easy to prepare and is especially attractive if a whole fish is used instead of fillets.

2   pounds 'ōpakapaka (pink snap-per), kajiki (Pacific blue marlin), halibut, salmon, or swordfish fillets (if using a whole dressed fish, allow ½ pound per person)

2   cups sliced citrus (select a mixture of lime, lemon, orange, kumquat)

4   tablespoons brandy or fruit juice

8   dill sprigs

Garnish: Reserve a few fresh fruit slices to dress the fish on the serving platter.

Place fillets or fish on heavy duty foil. Surround and top fish fillets with fruit slices and dill sprigs. If using a whole fish, stuff and top it with the fruit slices and dill. Pour on brandy. Wrap well, sealing the fish and the fruit in the foil. Grill over medium coals, allowing 10 minutes per inch for the thickness of the fish.

Oven method: Bake in the oven at 350°, allowing about 8 minutes per pound of fish. Test before the last 5 minutes to make certain that fish does not overcook. Remove to serving platter and garnish with fresh fruit slices.

Citrus Grilled Fish Steaks

Yield: 6 servings

⅓   cup lime juice

1   tablespoon honey

2   tablespoons sliced gingerroot

24 ounces fish fillets (1 inch thick)

Mix lime juice and honey with a wire whisk until blended. Add gingerroot. Refrigerate fillets in the sweet lime mixture at least 1 hour. Remove fish from the marinade. Discard ginger-root and bring marinade to a boil in a small saucepan. Boil 2 minutes. Coat grill rack with vegetable cooking spray. Grill fish steaks on prepared grill rack over medium-hot coals 8 minutes on each side or until fish flakes easily. Baste often with the marinade.

Chicken with Golden Orange (Kumquat)   Yield: 4 servings

1   tablespoon toasted sesame seeds

3   tablespoons Worcestershire sauce

¼   cup plum wine or fruit juice

2   teaspoons minced gingerroot

4   chicken breast halves, skinned and boned

1   teaspoon coarsely ground pepper

½   cup quartered kumquat pieces

¼   cup orange juice

Optional: Garnish with green onion strips and ½ teaspoon sesame oil.

Mix the first four ingredients in a medium-sized bowl and marinate chicken breasts in the refrigerator for 15 minutes or several hours. Lightly coat a wok or skillet with vegetable cooking spray. Remove chicken from marinade and place into prepared wok. Discard marinade. Add pepper to chicken and cook over medium heat 5 minutes per side or until done. Remove to serving platter. Place kumquats and orange juice in wok and barely warm. Do not cook. Spoon fruit and juice over chicken breasts.

Citrus Curry Chicken   Yield: 4 servings

This fast and easy recipe is a family dinner, yet it has a touch of the tropics. If time permits, bone chicken thighs.

2   pounds chicken thighs

1   (10¾-ounce) can condensed cream of chicken soup

1   tablespoon curry powder or to taste

1   tablespoon onion flakes

1   tablespoon minced parsley

1   teaspoon garlic powder

½   cup golden raisins

½   cup chopped peanuts

1   cup orange, tangerine, or grapefruit, coarsely chopped; or a mixture of fruits totaling 1 cup

Place thighs in baking pan. Thoroughly mix all ingredients and pour over thighs. Cover and bake at 350° 40 minutes or until chicken is completely done. Remove chicken to serving platter. Stir sauce smooth and serve over rice or chicken.

Microwave method: Arrange chicken in a 2-quart microwave-safe container. Thoroughly mix all ingredients and pour over thighs. Cover. Microwave at High 20 minutes or until chicken is completely cooked. Let stand covered 5 minutes before removing to serving platter. Stir sauce smooth and serve over rice or chicken.

Tropical Fruit Vodka

This recipe gives both unique tasting vodka and spirited fruit for dessert sauce or for fruity wine and vinegar.

Select from: Orange, tangerine, lime, lemon (deseeded and sliced); guava strips (deseeded), mango (peeled, deseeded, and sliced); pomegranate (puréed and strained), passion fruit (strained)

Vodka

Prick fruit slices to absorb liquid. Fill any size jar with prepared fruit. Cover with vodka and seal. Refrigerate 8 weeks turning upside down twice a week. Decant and strain the vodka into a suitable container. The fruit can be used to top ice cream, cake, and other desserts. The fruit can also flavor sherry, red or white wine, and vinegar. To make a fruity wine or vinegar, put the spirited fruit into a jar, add wine, sherry, or vinegar. Place it in the refrigerator to ripen for 2 weeks and turn it upside down twice a week. Decant the liquid and use within 6 weeks.

Sweet Lime Dressing

2   cups plain yogurt

½   cup lime juice

3   tablespoons dark honey

¼   cup lime zest

1   teaspoon caraway seeds

Yield: 2 cups

Mix all ingredients and chill thoroughly before serving. This is good with avocado and mixed fruit salads as well as with vegetable dishes.

Five-Star Fruit Dessert Sauce   Yield: 8 servings

This fresh fruit sauce is a blend of tropical flavors and gorgeous color. Serve it instead of frosting with chocolate and angel food cake and as a topping with lemon and orange sherbet.

2   cups orange cubes

3   cups mango cubes

1   cup strawberry slices

1   cup pineapple cubes

1/4 cup triple sec

1   unpeeled and minced lime

1/4 cup chopped mint leaves

Mix all ingredients together in a 2-quart container and refrigerate at least 2 hours to blend flavors. Refrigerate overnight to intensify flavors, but use within 48 hours for a fresh taste.

Citrus Muffins   Yield: 1 dozen

A brown sugar topping complements the fresh, tart flavor of these muffins.

2   cups all-purpose flour

2 1/2 teaspoons baking powder

1/2 teaspoon salt

1   teaspoon ground ginger

1/3 cup sugar

1   egg, beaten

2/3 cup milk

1/2 cup orange juice or tangerine juice

1/4 cup oil

1   tablespoon zest

1/4 cup brown sugar

Combine first five ingredients in large bowl. Make a well in the center of the mixture. Combine remaining ingredients, except brown sugar, and add to dry ingredients. Stir to moisten. Lightly coat spray muffin pans with vegetable cooking spray. Spoon batter into prepared muffin pans and press 1 teaspoon brown sugar into each muffin top. Bake at 375° for 15 minutes or until done. Remove muffins from pans immediately.

Citrus Butter

½ cup softened butter or margarine

3 tablespoons lime, orange, or grapefruit juice

1 tablespoon zest

Use a food processor or mixer to beat the ingredients until soft and light. This is good served with grilled fish, muffins, and pancakes.

Orange Acorn Squash

Yield: 4 servings

2 acorn squash, halved lengthwise, deseeded

1 cup orange chunks

⅓ cup pineapple tidbits, drained

3 tablespoons brown sugar

¼ cup margarine

½ teaspoon curry powder

Place squash halves hollow side up on microwave-safe plate. Cover squash loosely and microwave at High 8 minutes or until squash is barely tender. Mix the fruit and divide equally, filling squash halves. Combine remaining ingredients in a 1-cup glass measure and microwave at High 2 minutes or until bubbly. Drizzle warm mixture over fruit-filled squash. Cover loosely and microwave at High 3 minutes before serving.

Low-Cal Citrus Spinach Salad

Yield: 6 servings

1 cup grapefruit, pummelo, tangerine, or orange chunks
1/2 cup low-fat cottage cheese
1/2 teaspoon ground ginger
3 cups torn fresh spinach
3 cups torn iceberg lettuce
1/2 cup celery slices
1/4 cup unsalted sunflower kernels

Combine first three ingredients in container of food processor or electric blender and process with knife blade until smooth. Chill. Place torn spinach, lettuce, and celery in salad bowl and toss. Pour dressing over salad greens and sprinkle with sunflower kernels.

Orange Pound Cake

Yield: 1 loaf

1 3/4 cups sifted cake flour
2 teaspoons baking powder
1/4 teaspoon salt
1/2 teaspoon ground cardamom
3/4 cup sugar
1/2 cup vegetable oil
1 teaspoon lemon flavoring
1 teaspoon vanilla flavoring
1/2 cup unsweetened orange juice
1 tablespoon zest
4 egg whites, stiffly beaten

Combine first five ingredients in a large bowl. Add oil, flavorings, and orange juice. Beat at medium speed with electric mixer until batter is smooth and thick. Add zest and stir in one-third of egg whites. Fold in remaining egg whites. Coat 9 by 5-inch loaf pan with vegetable cooking spray. Pour batter into prepared pan. Bake at 350° for 45 minutes or until done. Cool in pan 10 minutes before removing to wire rack.

White Sangría Wedding Punch

Yield: 3 quarts

This special-occasion punch uses white wine for a different appearance from traditional red sangría.

1   (12-ounce) can frozen lemonade concentrate, thawed and undiluted

1   (6-ounce) can frozen orange juice concentrate, thawed and undiluted

1½ cups water

2   (750-milliliter) bottles dry white wine, chilled

2   (10-ounce) bottles club soda, chilled

Garnishes: Lemon, lime, and orange slices, unpeeled and deseeded.

Combine and freeze the first three ingredients until firm. To serve, spoon the frozen mixture into serving bowl. Add wine, soda, and garnishes.

Tangerine Carrots

Yield: 4 servings

1   tablespoon curry powder

¼   cup tangerine or other citrus fruit juice

3   cups ¼-inch carrot slices

1   green onion, diced

2   cups tangerine sections

½   teaspoon ground nutmeg

Place curry powder and tangerine juice in a wide skillet over medium heat. Stir to dissolve the curry powder. Add carrot slices, cover, and cook to tender crisp, about 3–5 minutes. Remove carrot slices with slotted spoon to serving dish. Add green onion and tangerine sections to the skillet and gently warm at low heat. Pour fruit mixture over the carrots and sprinkle with ground nutmeg.

Coconut

Cocos nucifera

THE COCONUT PALM continues to remain an enduring romantic symbol of the tropics, enticing artists, writers, travelers, and adventurers to the South Seas. The principal coconut-growing regions are within 22 degrees north or south of the equator. Hawai'i is near the northern limit for coconut growing, but many excellent varieties thrive although they do not bear as abundantly as they do farther south. Most varieties of coconuts now growing in Hawai'i were introduced within the last century. Early records indicate that the coconuts brought by ancient Polynesians on their migrations from the south were smaller.

The origin of the coconut is uncertain, but most likely it is from Melanesia or the shores of the Indian Ocean. Sanskrit for coconut tree is *kalpa vriksha*, the tree that produces all the necessities of life. Cocos and coconut are from the Portuguese for monkey, referring to the "eyes" of the coconut shell.

The coconut can grow spontaneously, as it has done on many atolls. Its buoyant husk and leathery outside skin enable it to float for 3–4 months in salt water and still germinate.

The coconut palm grows to eighty feet, bears fruit after 6–12 years, continues to bear for 100 years, and yields about fifty coconuts annually. Coconuts form continuously during the year. The coconut contains its maximum liquid of four cups at 4 months and reaches its full size at 5 1/2 months. As the nut matures, the meat forms around the inside of the shell. The thin, white, jellylike layer that forms first is called "spoon" coconut in Hawai'i, named for the utensil used to eat it. The meat hardens at about 7 months, with full maturity at 1 year when all the liquid has solidified into nut meat. Nuts fall from the tree at 14 months.

The fruit consists of four parts: husk, shell or nut, coconut water, and coconut meat. A ripe coconut is 35 percent husk, 12 percent shell,

25 percent water, and 28 percent meat. The oval coconut is six to twelve inches long, six to ten inches in diameter, and weighs seven to eight pounds.

Neither coconut water nor coconut milk (cream) is comparable to cow's milk. The translucent liquid, coconut water, in the cavity of the nut preserves the moisture of the coconut meat. Water taken from an uncontaminated nut is usually sterile. In emergencies during World War II, surgeons put coconut water directly into the patient's veins when sterile glucose was unavailable. Coconut milk, a creamy white liquid, is pressed from the meat of the ripe nut.

The coconut palm was a part of ancient Hawaiian culture. It supplied fruit for food and drink. The dried meat, copra, provided coconut oil when crushed. The husk provided coarse fibers for rope, leaf midribs became a broom, the hard shell served as a utensil as well as charcoal, and the swollen trunk base became the *pahu hula*, large hula drum.

There are still remnants of ancient Hawaiian coconut groves. Puna, on the Big Island, contains the largest continuous groves in the Islands. Others are at Hōnaunau and Laupāhoehoe on the Big Island; at Waihe'e, Wailua Nui, and Mākena on Maui; at Pōka'ī and Punalu'u on O'ahu; at Wailua (famous sacred grove), Kōloa, Hanalei, and Hā'ena on Kaua'i; and at Wailua and on Moloka'i.

Use

When selecting a ripe nut in the market, shake it and choose only those with a good quantity of juice. Refrigerated coconuts will keep for 1 month. Ripe nuts in the market are sold husked. If nuts need husking, it can be a hard task. It is frequently done by planting a pick into the ground with the point up, grasping the coconut with both hands, and removing the husk by driving it onto the sharp point. An expert can remove the husk in three to four pieces in 30 seconds.

To get the coconut water from a ripe nut, pierce the "embryo eye," the soft one, with a nail or an ice pick and drain. Heat the nut in the oven at 375° for 10 minutes or freeze the coconut for about an hour to facilitate cracking. Hold the nut with a towel and crack it around the circumference with a hammer. Pry out the flesh and cut into chunks; these can be shredded, sliced, or grated in a food processor. A vegetable peeler will remove the brown skin from the coconut meat, but this is not necessary if making coconut milk, which will be strained.

To make coconut milk, combine equal parts of boiling water or boiling coconut water with coconut meat in a food processor. Grind the meat to fine using a metal blade. Pour into sieve or colander lined with dampened cheesecloth. Drain milk. Press and twist cloth to extract more liquid from coconut meat. Repeat with remaining coconut meat and boiling water. An average coconut yields 3 cups of milk. Refrigerate up to 2 days or store in freezer for months. If allowed to stand, a concentrate will separate from the milk and can be whipped. Don't boil coconut milk because it curdles. Coconut milk, not coconut water, is high in saturated fat (25–35 percent) and should be used sparingly in the diet. Commercially frozen coconut milk is an acceptable substitute in all recipes.

Hawaiians add coconut milk to cooked chicken, fish, or taro leaves near the end of the cooking process. They also make a coconut pudding called *haupia* that is frequently served at lū'aus (celebrations). Polynesians combine the milk with bananas, breadfruit, sweet potatoes, and taro in baked or steamed puddings. Coconut milk can be added to curries and combined with puréed fruits in frozen desserts.

Grated or shredded coconut is used in cakes, bread, curry, vegetable dishes, fruit salad, shrimp dishes, and chicken dishes. Freshly grated coconut keeps for 3–4 days or can be frozen and stored in airtight containers at least a year. Because coconut is high in fat, it is best reserved for special occasions.

To toast coconut in the microwave, spread $1/3$ cup coconut in a 9-inch pie plate and cook at High $1–1\frac{1}{2}$ minutes or until golden. Alternate method: Spread coconut in a shallow pan. Bake at 350° until lightly brown, about 20 minutes.

☀☀☀☀☀☀☀

Green Coconut Cooler

Select a half-mature green coconut. Remove the husk, leaving a section on the base. Cut the base flat so that the nut stands upright. Chill. To serve, make holes through the two eyes and insert a straw. Or cut off the top and serve with a straw. This is a delicious and refreshing drink.

Coconut Party Cake

Prepare a yellow or a white cake mix following package instructions for a three-layer cake. Use guava filling I or II and toasted coconut frosting for an elegant dessert. Guava purée produces the strongest fresh fruit flavor. Cake assembly: Lightly brush loose crumbs from top and sides. Place three to four strips of wax paper over the edges of the cake serving plate. Place the first layer bottom side up. Spread on guava filling. Place the next layer top side up and spread on guava filling. Repeat for top layer. Spread a thin layer of frosting on the sides to set any crumbs. Frost the sides and then the top. Pull out wax paper.

If the frosting is a creamy type, it will freeze up to 3 months. Place the cake, uncovered, in the freezer for several hours until it is frozen. Wrap in foil loosely but completely and return to freezer. To thaw, unwrap cake immediately upon removal from freezer and let stand at room temperature for 2–3 hours.

✳✳✳✳✳✳✳

Guava Filling I

1   cup guava fruit spread or jam

1   tablespoon cornstarch

1   tablespoon water

1   tablespoon triple sec

1/2 cup shredded coconut

Place guava spread into a saucepan and bring to a boil over medium heat. Mix cornstarch, water, and triple sec and add to guava spread. Stir in the coconut. Cook, stirring until mixture returns to a boil and thickens. Remove from heat and cool.

Guava Filling II

When cream cheese is used in a filling or frosting, keep the cake refrigerated.

1   (8-ounce) package low-fat cream cheese, softened

1/2 cup guava purée

2   tablespoons honey

1/2 cup shredded coconut

Combine ingredients.

Variation: Substitute 1/4 cup guava juice for purée and omit honey.

Easy Toasted Coconut Frosting

Purchase 3 cups of prepared white frosting or prepare your favorite recipe. Add 1 cup toasted, shredded coconut.

Cool and Crispy Coconut Pie with Coconut Crumb Crust

Yield: 9-inch pie

1   cup shredded coconut
½   cup gingersnap crumbs
½   cup graham cracker crumbs
¼   cup melted butter

Combine all ingredients and mix. Firmly press mixture over bottom and ¾ inch up sides of 9-inch pie pan. Bake at 350° for 5 minutes. Chill. Fill cool crust with 1 quart of either rocky road or mint-chocolate chip ice cream, softened. Cover pie with wax paper and freeze until firm. Let ice cream pie stand at room temperature 5 minutes before serving.

Alternate filling: This crust makes an attractive holiday pie when filled with instant pistachio pudding and pie filling. Top pie with ⅓ cup toasted coconut.

Coconut 'n Oats Bars

Yield: 2 dozen

2¼ cups quick-cooking oats, uncooked
1   cup shredded coconut
¼   cup wheat germ
¼   cup butter
¼   cup brown sugar
¼   cup honey
¼   cup peanut butter
1   tablespoon vanilla extract
½   cup chopped unsalted peanuts
½   cup raisins

Lightly coat a 9-inch square baking pan with vegetable cooking spray. Combine oats, coconut, and wheat germ in prepared pan. Bake at 325° for 15 minutes, stirring occasionally. Set aside. Combine butter, brown sugar, and honey in a medium saucepan; cook over medium heat, stirring occasionally, until butter melts and brown sugar dissolves. Remove from heat; add peanut butter and vanilla. Stir until peanut butter melts and pour over the oats mixture. Add peanuts and raisins. Stir until moist. Press mixture into pan. Bake at 350° for 12 minutes or until done.

Guava

Psidium guajava

GUAVAS ARE THE MOST COMMON wild fruit in Hawai'i. Although they are available from April to October, about one-third of the crop comes in the spring and the remaining two-thirds in the fall. Guava was introduced to Hawai'i about 1800 by Don Francisco de Paula Marin, the horticulturist who brought countless fruit specimens from many places to the Islands. The guava immediately escaped to become a pest in some areas.

Along with the aromatic clove, eucalpytus, and allspice, the guava is a member of the myrtle family (Myrtaceae). Guava, from the Haitian *guayaba*, is a shrublike evergreen tree growing from a few feet to thirty feet, bearing at 18 months, and continuing to fruit for 40 years. The three- to six-inch, blunt leaves are slightly hairy underneath. The white and yellow guava flower is subtly fragrant.

The intrepid Spanish and Portuguese are responsible for spreading guavas worldwide. One hundred fifty species of guavas, which originated in the American tropics between Mexico and Peru, now grow wild in frost-free areas throughout the world from 27 degrees north latitude to 30 degrees south latitude. Guavas currently grow in Florida, California, Arizona, Australia, India, South Africa, the Caribbean, and Southeast Asia.

One variety of guava, called the "apple of the tropics," is a dessert guava. This low-acid, high-sugar guava is popular in India, Indonesia, and Thailand and is eaten half ripe while still crunchy. Gardeners can produce it in Hawai'i by growing Hong Kong Pink, Ruby Supreme, or Holmberg.

Another kind of guava, the strawberry guava (*Psidium cattleianum*), is frequently found by hikers in Hawai'i. This sweet, yet tangy, fruit is called "cherry guava" in some parts of the world. It does not taste like either a cherry or a strawberry. The fruit is red-purple, round, and about 1 inch in diameter, with white flesh and many seeds. It is used for jam or as a thirst quencher, but should not be substituted for *Psidium guajava* in recipes. There is also a yellow strawberry guava *(P. cattleianum* var. *lucidum)* that bears a slightly larger fruit.

Botanically, guava is classified as a berry and varies widely in form, color, shape, size, sweetness, and seed content. The fruit is oval or round and one to four inches in diameter. The edible skin is yellow-green and, occasionally, almost white or red. The flesh is white, light yellow, or pink and some types of guava even have red or orange flesh. The small, hard, white seeds are held in the center of the fruit by a jellylike pulp. Many guavas have excessive seeds, but some, like the Beaumont, have few. The Aztec name for guava is *xalxocotl*, meaning "sand plum," which describes the texture of puréed guava.

Guava ranks first in fruit production on Kaua'i and follows pineapple, papaya, and banana in fruit production value statewide. Kīlauea, Kaua'i, the "guava capital of the World," has Beaumont guava orchards in commercial cultivation. The large and luscious Beaumont, although not sweet, has pulp that is a gorgeous, strawberry ice cream pink. During harvest, these trees may require picking thirty-five times because the fruit does not ripen uniformly.

Use

Guavas bruise easily when ripe. Select mature green-stage guavas and they will keep for a week under refrigeration. When ready to use, ripen at room temperature 1–5 days. At the ripe stage, guavas will keep only a day or two under refrigeration.

Use the whole fruit because a large proportion of vitamin C is concentrated in the edible rind. Guava has five times the vitamin C content of an orange, and some authorities believe it has ten times that amount.

Cooking with guava is a joy. The fragrant aroma is fresh and spicy. Use guava purée in stew, soup, salad dressing, fruit sauce, catsup, vinegar, marinade, and bread. It can be thinned for cake icing or added to pudding. It makes a beautiful mousse, sorbet, and ice cream. Guava purée enriches a stew, soup, or curry, making it thicker and giving it a subtle flavor. Guava's high pectin content makes it ideal for jam and marmalade. Combined with another fruit, guava makes nutritious, delightful fruitsicles.

Do not peel guava. The rind can be puréed along with the pulp. If only the flesh is puréed, use the shell halves in jam, chutney, or bread. The shells can be cut into strips or minced and used in many recipes.

To remove seeds from the pulp, use a colander or sieve and mash the pulp along the sides. Seeds remain while the pulp passes through into the bowl. A foodmill is also suitable for removing guava seeds. Purée can be frozen in ice cube trays and then put into freezer bags. Both guava shells and pulp freeze well for at least 1 year.

To purée guava: Place unpeeled fruit chunks including seeds in food processor. Process with knife blade until guava resembles the texture of applesauce. Strain purée with sieve to remove seeds. Purée can be frozen up to 6 months. Guava pulp is tart, but exquisite, over fruit salads, cakes, ice cream, and sorbet.

❊❊❊❊❊❊❊

Devilish Decadent Chocolate Cake

Yield: 12 servings

1   (18 ½-ounce) package devil's food cake mix

6   ounces semisweet chocolate chips

½   cup rum or guava juice

½   cup guava jam or strawberry jam

Frosting:

6   ounces semisweet chocolate chips

1   cup sour cream

Lightly coat with vegetable cooking spray two 9-inch cake pans. Prepare cake mix as directed and add 6 ounces of chocolate chips to the batter. Spoon into prepared cake pans. Bake at 350° for 30 to 35 minutes. Cool 5 minutes on wire rack before removing cake from pans. Brush cake tops with rum. Cool. Place one layer on serving platter and spread top with guava jam. To make the frosting, melt remaining 6 ounces of chocolate chips in microwave at Medium for 3 minutes. Stir in sour cream until smooth and creamy. Assemble layers, frosting only the top and sides. Refrigerate at least 15 minutes before serving. Cake freezes for up to 1 week.

Hawaiian Sunset Salad

Yield: 4 servings

In Hawai'i, many people watch sunsets carefully, looking for a "green flash" on the horizon as the sun's ball of fire sinks into the beautiful, blue Pacific. This salad, combining green, gold, pink, yellow, and red, carries with it the memory of a Hawaiian sunset.

3 cups Chinese pea pods

2 guavas, unpeeled, deseeded, and diced

1 carambola, thin star slices

1/2 cup sliced water chestnuts

1/2 cup thinly sliced red onion

3 cups coarsely chopped watercress

Dressing:

4 tablespoons macadamia or olive oil

1 tablespoon coarse black pepper

2 kumquats, minced or 2 tablespoons lime zest

1 tablespoon sesame seeds

Optional: The addition of 3 cups cooked chicken cubes turns this salad into a meal.

Steam or microwave pea pods to crunchy but tender. Cool. Mix dressing ingredients in salad bowl. Toss pea pods and all remaining ingredients with the dressing in salad bowl. Cover and chill at least 30 minutes.

Guava Brunch Soup

Yield: 6 servings

3 cups tomato juice

2 cups guava purée

1 cup nonfat chicken broth

1/2 cup dry sherry

1 cup whipped, skimmed evaporated milk

Garnish: 1/2 cup green onion, finely chopped

Combine all ingredients except evaporated milk in a large pan over low heat. Mix thoroughly. When heated through, fold in whipped milk. Serve warm in cups or individual soup bowls garnished with green onion.

Guava Party Salad

Yield: 6 servings

Pastry salad bowl:

2/3 cup water

1/4 cup vegetable oil

2/3 cup flour

1 egg

3 egg whites

Filling:

4 cups cooked teriyaki beef or cooked roast beef, julienne strips

3 cups coarsely chopped watercress or red lettuce

1 sweet red pepper, thinly sliced

1/2 cup diced, canned bamboo shoots

1/2 cup thinly sliced sweet, red onion

1 cup lychee halves

1 cup guava, unpeeled, deseeded, and minced

1 cup julienne cucumber slices

Dressing:

1/2 cup plain yogurt

1/2 cup avocado purée

1/4 cup guava purée

1 tablespoon prepared mustard

1/2 teaspoon dried tarragon

Salt and coarse pepper to taste

In a 2-quart pan, combine water and oil and bring to boil. Add flour and stir until dough holds together. Fit food processor with knife blade and place dough into the container. Add egg and egg whites, processing to smooth. Lightly coat 9-inch cake pan with removable rim with vegetable cooking spray. Scrape dough into prepared cake pan and smooth it over bottom and sides. Bake at 400° about 40 minutes or until pastry is puffed and golden. Turn off oven and pierce pastry about 12 times in several places. Leave pastry in closed oven to dry for 10 minutes. Remove from pan and cool completely. Can be wrapped and frozen for 2 weeks. To recrisp, heat crust at 350° for 10 minutes. Cool thoroughly before filling.

Combine all filling ingredients in large bowl and toss gently. Blend dressing ingredients in small bowl. Pour dressing over salad and toss. To serve, place pastry bowl onto serving platter and fill with salad. This salad is a showy luncheon entrée.

Guava Catsup

Yield: 6 cups

5 tablespoons pickling spice
1 tablespoon chopped gingerroot
1 red onion
2–3 small chilies or to taste
6 cups guava or carambola purée
1/2 cup vinegar
1 cup brown sugar
1 cinnamon stick
1 teaspoon ground allspice
1 tablespoon celery seeds
2 tablespoons ground cloves
Zest from 1 orange

Place first four ingredients in food processor or blender container and use knife blade to chop finely. Place purée in large pan and add all ingredients. Simmer over low heat to thicken for about 30 minutes, stirring frequently to avoid sticking. Pour into hot, sterilized jars or freezer bags. Seal, cool, and refrigerate for up to 2 months or freeze up to 6 months. This tart condiment is good with chicken, turkey, and ham sandwiches. It makes a unique sauce to serve with fish, roast, and chops.

Microwave method: Place one-half the prepared mixture in a pourable 2-quart glass measure. Cover loosely and microwave at High 10 minutes or until thick. Repeat for remaining ingredients.

Guava Barbecue Sauce

Yield: 4 cups

2 cups guava purée
1 thumb fresh gingerroot, finely chopped
1 (4-ounce) can diced green chilies
2 cloves garlic, finely chopped
1 cup soy sauce
1 cup catsup
1/4 cup olive oil

Thoroughly blend all ingredients. To intensify flavors, refrigerate at least 1 hour. Refrigerate up to 1 week or freeze up to 3 months. Good with all grilled meats and seafood.

Guava Fruit Spread

Yield: 4 cups

Avoid a hot-bath treatment and the use of paraffin for this jamlike product by freezing or refrigerating it. Do not store fruit spread at room temperature. Because this method requires little cooking time, it has both excellent texture and color, with a tart, fresh flavor. Guava fruit spread can be made without honey. For a sweeter spread, add honey before serving.

4¹/₂ cups coarsely chopped guavas, unpeeled and deseeded

1 package of fruit pectin for light jam

4 tablespoons concentrated guava, pineapple, or passion fruit juice

1 tablespoon pumpkin pie spice

Optional: 3 tablespoons honey.

Place all ingredients into a 3- to 4-quart saucepan over medium heat. Stir to dissolve and boil 1 minute while stirring constantly. Remove fruit spread from heat. Pour into sterilized containers or freezer bags. Cool at room temperature 24 hours and then freeze up to 6 months or refrigerate up to 3 months.

To make "Hot Guava" jam, mix these ingredients into the fruit pulp and follow fruit pectin for light jam directions:

3 tiny red chilies, minced, or 2 tablespoons chopped green chilies

1 teaspoon coriander seeds

¹/₂ teaspoon cumin seeds

¹/₂ teaspoon cardamom seeds

Guava Chutney

Yield: approximately 6 pints

2 cups cider vinegar

1 cup brown sugar

7 cups chopped guavas, unpeeled and deseeded

1 cup chopped red apple, unpeeled and deseeded

1 cup strawberry slices

1 cup chopped red onion

1 cinnamon stick

1 tablespoon ground cinnamon

1 tablespoon ground nutmeg

1 tablespoon ground mace

1 tablespoon ground ginger

1 tablespoon coriander seeds

1/4 cup chopped fresh gingerroot

Dissolve vinegar and brown sugar over medium heat in a large pan. Add remaining ingredients. Simmer and stir constantly. The chutney can be cooked to desired consistency over low heat about thirty minutes or finished in the microwave. Pour or spoon into sterilized jars or freezer bags. Cool guava chutney at room temperature. Refrigerate the chutney up to 1 month or freeze up to 3 months. Serve this chutney with poultry and seafood dishes. Mix it with salad dressings for unique salads, and mix it with strawberry or chocolate ice cream for an unusual flavor.

Microwave method: Place 4 cups of the chutney mixture into a 2-quart pourable glass measure. Microwave at High about ten minutes or to desired consistency, stirring every 3 minutes. Repeat procedure for remaining ingredients.

Dessert Guava Sauce

Sweeten guava purée with jam, honey, brown sugar, or a liqueur. Use 2 tablespoons of sweetener per 1 cup of purée and add flavor with 1/2 teaspoon apple pie spice per 1 cup of purée. To warm sauce, place 1 cup of guava sauce in the microwave at High 2–3 minutes or on the stove top for 1 minute. Do not boil. This is good on lemon or pineapple sorbet, strawberry ice cream, angel food cake, and gingerbread.

Sourdough Guava Bread

Yield: 16 servings

Breads are one of man's earliest foods. The Egyptians were among the first to make flat cakes from a flour-and-water dough baked without leaven. The discovery of fermented bread is attributed to them. They used the leaven of sour dough, left from previous bread-making, together with fermented grape juice processed for wine. The dough was kneaded and dried in the sun.

Sourdough starter:

1   cup warm water

1/4   cup plain low-fat yogurt

1   cup all-purpose flour

Batter:

1   cup all-purpose flour

1   cup wheat bran cereal

1/2   cup whole-wheat flour

1/3   cup sugar

1   teaspoon baking soda

1/4   teaspoon salt

1/2   teaspoon ground cardamom

1/2   cup sourdough starter

1/4   cup melted margarine

3   tablespoons molasses

1   egg, beaten

1   cup guava purée or banana purée

Combine water and yogurt. Pour into a 2-quart glass container and cover loosely with plastic wrap. Let stand at about 85° for 24 hours. Gradually stir in flour until blended. Cover and let stand at about 85° for 72 hours, stirring the mixture two or three times a day. Refrigerate the mixture and stir once a day. Use it within 11 days.

To use starter: Remove from refrigerator and let stand at room temperature 1 hour. Stir and measure amount needed for recipe. Replenish leftover starter with 3/4 cup flour and 3/4 cup warm water. Return to refrigerator. Use within 11 days, stirring daily.

To make bread: Lightly coat a 9 by 5 by 3-inch loaf pan with vegetable cooking spray. Combine first seven batter ingredients in large bowl. Combine starter and next 3 ingredients in separate bowl. Mix well and add to dry ingredients. Stir well. Fold in the purée and spoon it into prepared pan. Bake at 375° for 55–60 minutes or until done. Cool in pan 10 minutes. Remove from pan and cool on wire rack.

Island Party Punch

Yield: 4 quarts

1   (12-ounce) can guava–passion fruit frozen concentrate juice

2   cups unsweetened pineapple juice

½   cup lime juice

2   cups guava, pineapple, or papaya purée

3   tablespoons grenadine syrup

7   cups strong mint or fruit tea

3   (28-ounce) bottles ginger ale, chilled

Ice block

Optional: Replace ice block and grenadine syrup with half gallon tangerine, lemon, or pineapple sherbet.

Combine all ingredients except ginger ale and ice. Chill thoroughly. Add mixture to punch bowl and blend. Add ice block and chilled ginger ale.

Pink Guava Margarita Sorbet

Yield: 6 cups

1   cup water

½   cup sugar

2   cups fresh strawberries

1½ cups guava purée

¼   cup orange-flavored liqueur

6   tablespoons tequila

Combine water and sugar in small saucepan and boil, stirring constantly until sugar dissolves. Cool. Purée strawberries using knife blade in food processor. Combine all remaining ingredients except tequila. Pour sorbet mixture into freezer can of a 6-cup ice cream freezer. Freeze according to manufacturer's instructions. Before serving, top each scoop of sorbet with 1 tablespoon tequila.

Alternate method: Pour mixture into 13 by 9 by 2-inch pan. Freeze until almost firm. Break mixture into large pieces and process in food processor using knife blade until fluffy, but not thawed. Refreeze until firm.

Frozen Yogurt Guava Pops

Yield: 8 pops

1½ cups guava purée

2 cups mashed banana

1 cup plain or fruit-flavored yogurt

Wooden popsicle sticks and 3-ounce paper cups or commercial kit

Place all ingredients into a blender or food processor. Mix. Pour equal amounts into paper cups. Freeze partially. Insert wooden sticks and freeze until firm. Or follow instructions with plastic commercial kit. Yogurt pops can be wrapped tightly and frozen for up to 1 month. This popular, nutritious snack is enjoyed at breakfast or any time by children and adults. Using a fruit-flavored yogurt produces a sweeter popsicle. Experiment using a variety of flavored yogurts. Piña colada and strawberry flavors are particularly good.

Lychee

Litchi chinensis

O F ALL TROPICAL FRUITS, the reputation of the lychee is the most sensuous. The first Chinese fruit culture book, written in 1056, was about the lychee. This fruit has been esteemed and enjoyed in the Orient for over 2,000 years.

Lady Yang Kuei Fei so loved lychee that T'ang Emperor Hsüan Tsung (A.D. 712–756) organized a "pony express" to carry lychee 500 miles on horseback from hot, southern Kwangtung (Guangdong) to the northern court for her. Lychees have been cultivated for thousands of years and, in addition to China, they are also grown in Thailand, the Philippines, Taiwan, India, South Africa, Australia, and several places in the United States. When the first boat brought Chinese contract laborers to the sugar plantations in Hawai'i in 1852, lychee was one of the Oriental fruit trees on board as well as longan, pummelo, and mandarin orange.

The lychee tree is very sensitive to frost, drought, and wind. Its flowers are small and green-white. It can grow to fifty feet, begins bearing after 5–10 years, reaches its prime in 20–30 years, and may continue producing for 50 years (some sources say a thousand years). In 1980, a lychee tree, supposedly planted in the eighth century A.D., was found in Fukien Province in China, still bearing. The characteristics of the parent plant can be maintained through asexual propagation, using air layering. If this was done, the age is feasible.

In Hawai'i, good trees can bear 200 or more pounds of fruit from May to July. Fruits grow in clusters, are oval or round, and are about one inch in size. The brittle, inedible, rough, reddish shell peels easily to reveal the lychee's pearly white, translucent flesh. It has a dark brown, inedible seed. The flesh of a fresh lychee is fragrant, sweet, and juicy, making a grape seem very bland.

Many years ago, when the fruit was first available on the American mainland, it was dried. The outside of a peeled and dried lychee resembles a nut shell and the fruit was called "lychee nut." The chewy texture and smoky taste of this dried fruit, similar to a raisin, have nothing in common with fresh lychee. Canned lychees, however, do retain some flavor of the fresh fruit and can be used successfully in recipes.

Use

Select the heaviest and fullest fruit with stems. Red fruit is fresh. Even fresh fruit with brown spots on the shell are delicious as long as the shell is not cracked or shriveled. Lychee keeps 2 weeks when refrigerated and about 6 months frozen. Freeze lychee unpeeled in freezer bags or freezer containers. Occasionally, the lychee shell cracks during freezing, but the fruit's flavor and texture remains good. Defrost lychee for easier peeling.

Fresh lychee is so exceptional and delicious that it almost seems improper to mix it with other fruit in a salad or dessert rather than serve it intact along with the delicate branches and leaves. Peel fruit from the stem down to keep it whole.

A lychee connoisseur could never purée a fresh lychee, but would substitute juice from the canned fruit. It is fragrant and will add flavor to gelatin, ice cream, salad dressing, or sauce. Lychee gives a gourmet touch to fruit and green salad, and turkey, ham, and chicken salad. Probably the most common use for lychee in Hawai'i is to stuff it for *pūpū* (appetizer).

❖❖❖❖❖❖

Stuffed Lychees

Yield: about 12 servings

¼ cup low-fat cream cheese, softened

¼ cup blue cheese, softened

1 tablespoon kirsch, port wine, or lychee juice from can

1 (20-ounce) can whole lychees or 20 fresh or frozen lychees, deseeded

Garnish: Paprika or minced parsley

Optional: ¼ cup finely chopped macadamia nuts.

Blend the cheeses, liquid, and nuts to a creamy consistency.

To stuff lychees: Drain canned lychees, reserving juice for another use. Remove excess liquid from lychees with a paper towel before stuffing. Place approximately 1 teaspoon of the cheese filling inside each lychee, filling it to the top. Level cheese filling at the top and wipe sides clean of filling. Sprinkle garnish on tops of stuffed lychees. Chill at least 1 hour before serving.

Tropical Chow Mein Salad

Yield: 8 servings

1   (20-ounce) can whole lychees or
    20 fresh or frozen lychees,
    deseeded

3   passion fruit or ¼ cup fresh
    lime juice

1   teaspoon honey

2   tablespoons dark rum

½   cup lychee juice from can or ½
    cup guava or pineapple juice

2   cups papaya or pineapple chunks

1   cup kiwi slices

1½ cups banana chunks

¼   cup preserved or candied ginger

Garnish: 1 (8-ounce) can chow mein
    noodles

Drain lychees and refrigerate the fruit, reserving juice. Open passion fruit, scoop out pulp, and place it with honey, rum, and lychee juice over low heat to loosen seeds. Sieve to remove seeds and refrigerate the dressing. Combine all salad ingredients in a large bowl. Pour on chilled dressing and re-frigerate at least 2 hours. Garnish salad with noodles before serving.

Fast Lychee Chocolate Sauce

Yield: 2 cups

1   (20-ounce) can whole lychees or
    15 fresh or frozen lychees,
    deseeded

6   ounces semisweet chocolate
    morsels

Optional: Add 1 tablespoon amaretto
    to sauce before serving. When
    using fresh or frozen lychees, ½
    cup juice from canned pears or
    fruit cocktail can replace the
    canned lychee juice.

Drain canned lychees, reserving juice. Cut lychee into halves. Place juice into 2-quart pourable glass measure and microwave at High 2 minutes. Add chocolate morsels and stir. Microwave at Medium High 2 minutes or until chocolate softens. Add lychee halves to chocolate sauce. Stir to mix. This rich sauce is wonderful on angel food cake, vanilla ice cream, and lemon and passion fruit sherbets.

Stove method: Melt chocolate morsels in juice over low heat. Add lychee halves and stir to warm.

Chicken and Lychees

Yield: 4 servings

1 (20-ounce) can lychees
2 tablespoons toasted sesame seeds
1 tablespoon honey
1/2 teaspoon poultry seasoning
4 (6-ounce) skinned chicken breast halves

To toast sesame seeds: Place 1/4 cup of seeds in a microwave-safe bowl at High 3 minutes; stir twice.

Drain lychees, reserving 1/4 cup juice and refrigerating remaining juice for another use. Set lychees aside. Mix 1/4 cup lychee juice, sesame seeds, honey, and poultry seasoning in a small bowl. Lightly coat rack and broiler pan with vegetable cooking spray. Place chicken on prepared broiler rack and brush it with lychee juice mixture. Broil eight inches from heat for 10 minutes, basting often with lychee juice mixture. Turn chicken, baste, and broil an additional 8 minutes or until done. Dip lychees into basting mixture and broil the last 2 minutes. Discard remaining basting mixture. Transfer chicken and lychees to serving platter.

Waikīkī Duck

Yield: 2 servings

Famous for its beautiful beaches and fashionable hotels, Waikīkī, meaning "spouting water," had springs, swamp water, and many duck ponds before it was drained in the 1920s by the construction of the Ala Wai Canal.

1 duck, dressed and quartered
2 tablespoons paprika
1/4 cup dry sherry or fruit juice
1 tablespoon minced parsley
1 teaspoon basil
1 teaspoon ground pepper
1 cup sliced fresh mushrooms
1 tablespoon arrowroot mixed with 2 tablespoons water
1 sweet red pepper, julienne strips
1 cup lychee halves, drained
1/2 cup tangerine segments, deseeded
Garnish: 1/2 cup macadamia nut bits

Trim all visible fat from duck. Lightly coat wok or skillet with vegetable cooking spray. Place prepared wok over medium heat and add paprika. Sear duck pieces until brown, about 5 minutes. Drain all fat from skillet before adding sherry and the next four ingredients. Cover and simmer duck 30 minutes or until done. Remove duck to serving platter. Stir arrowroot mixture into pan juices and cook over medium heat until smooth. Add remaining ingredients, cover, and cook 3 minutes. Do not overcook. Pour fruit sauce over duck and garnish.

Lychee Ice Cream

Yield: 12 servings

1   (20-ounce) can lychees

One-half gallon vanilla ice milk or rich French vanilla ice cream

1   tablespoon almond extract

Optional: 1/4 cup shredded coconut; 1/4 cup chopped nuts

Drain lychees and reserve juice. Cut whole lychees into halves and combine with 3 tablespoons of the drained juice. Save remaining juice for other uses. Add the lychees and almond flavoring to the softened ice cream. Mix and refreeze. The taste and texture of this wonderful ice cream served in chilled, stemmed glasses are incomparable and unattainable in a commercial product.

Lychee Champagne Punch

Yield: 6 quarts

1/4   cup honey

3   cups boiling water

3   cups papaya purée

2   (20-ounce) cans lychees and juice

1   (12-ounce) can frozen passion fruit juice concentrate, thawed and undiluted

1   (6-ounce) can frozen lemonade concentrate, thawed and undiluted

3   (750-milliliter) bottles chilled champagne

Garnish: Mint sprigs

Combine honey and boiling water, thoroughly dissolving honey. Cool. Combine honey mixture with remaining ingredients except champagne.

Pour into a large container and freeze firm. To serve, partially thaw frozen mixture, place it into punch bowl, and break it into chunks. Add chilled champagne. Stir gently until slushy. Garnish.

Lychees and Champagne

Yield: 6 servings

6   lychees, deseeded

6   raspberries or 6 maraschino cherries

1   bottle champagne

Chill all ingredients. Stuff each lychee with a raspberry. Place a stuffed lychee into a stemmed glass and fill with champagne. Serve immediately. This drink is a grand finale.

Macadamia Nut

Macadamia integrifolia

MACADAMIA, ONE OF THE WORLD'S FINEST NUTMEATS, is indigenous to the Australian rain forests of Queensland and northern New South Wales. It is named for John Macadam, an Australian chemist.

The macadamia nut came to Hawai'i in 1882 when William Purvis brought seeds from Australia and eventually planted seedling trees at Kukuihaele above Waipi'o Valley on the Big Island. One of those trees is 100 years old, still alive, and bearing. In 1918, the macadamia industry in Hawai'i began when Pierre Naquin, manager of Honoka'a Sugar Company, used seed from the Purvis trees to develop and plant 18,000 macadamia seedlings on Honoka'a land. At the outset, nuts were husked with a makeshift device utilizing a car's rear wheel. Later, modified pecan cracking machines were used.

On O'ahu, E. W. Jordan planted macadamia in Nu'uanu in 1890 and shortly thereafter planted 2,000 trees on Tantalus. Other trees were planted in Kona, on Kaua'i, and on Maui. Today, macadamia is the third most important agricultural commodity in the state, exceeded only by sugar and pineapple.

Macadamia is a member of the protea family (Proteaceae). It is a beautiful tree with creamy white flowers and hollylike lustrous, green, spiny leaves. The tree can reach sixty feet with a spread of forty feet. The fruit has a green, fleshy husk that splits open when the nuts are ripe. Inside is a hard-shelled, round seed enclosing a kernel, the macadamia nut.

Grafted trees bear in 3–4 years, but seedlings take at least 7 years. Macadamia produces for 65 years or longer and reaches full production at 14 years, which in Hawai'i is 100–107 pounds per tree. The yield per tree increases yearly to 100–150 pounds at 20 years. It takes 10–12 years to recapture the original costs of starting a commercial orchard, which partially explains the expensive price of macadamia nuts.

The nut crop in Hawai'i can ripen in both autumn and spring or throughout the year. When nuts are ripe, they fall to the ground. Their shells are extremely hard to crack, and it is necessary to use more than a regular commercial nut cracker. It takes 300 pounds per square inch of pressure to break the shell. There are both rough and smooth shell types, but the smooth-shell macadamia is the one in production in Hawai'i.

Use

Macadamia nuts impart a rich flavor to stuffing, breads, cakes, pie crust, and dessert topping. Macadamia nuts are good fresh or roasted. To roast nuts: Place nutmeats into a shallow pan with only two layers of nuts at 250° and roast until they are a dark cream color. Or use a microwave and place 1 1/2 cups of nuts into a 9-inch glass pie plate, heat at High for 3–4 minutes, and stir twice during the process. Lightly salt if desired.

Macadamia nut oil is a relatively new product. It is currently produced in Hawai'i, Australia, and South Africa. Because it is a vegetable oil, it is cholesterol free; it has 120 calories per tablespoon and is 80 percent monounsaturated. Its high smoke point makes it desirable for use in stir-fry cooking, and it does not lose flavor at a high temperature. The unique nutty, rich flavor of this oil makes it superb for salad dressings, marinade, barbecue sauce, and especially good for searing fish or sautéing shrimp. Its delicate flavor lingers on the palate.

❊❊❊❊❊❊❊

Mahimahi with Macadamia Sauce   Yield: 6 servings

Macadamia nuts give a gourmet touch to this easily prepared entrée.

6	(4-ounce) mahimahi fillets or other firm, white fish
1	tablespoon macadamia oil
1/2	cup fine whole-wheat breadcrumbs
1	tablespoon lime zest
1/4	cup sour cream
2	tablespoons Dijon mustard
1/2	cup macadamia nut bits

Brush fillets with macadamia oil. Toss bread crumbs and lime zest. Lightly coat 12 by 8 by 2-inch baking dish with vegetable cooking spray. Dredge fillets in breadcrumbs and arrange in a single layer in prepared baking dish. Bake uncovered at 500° for 10 minutes or until fish flakes easily. Transfer fillets to serving platter. Mix sour cream and mustard in small saucepan. Cook over low heat to warm, but do not boil. Evenly divide sauce and macadamia nuts over fillets.

Macadamia Ice Cream Pie

Yield: 9-inch pie

This layered ice cream treat features a crunchy toffee filling with a crisp, nutty crust.

1 egg white (at room temperature)

1/4 cup sugar

1 1/2 cups macadamia nut bits

2 (1 1/8-ounce) toffee-flavored candy bars

1 quart macadamia ice cream

Lightly coat 9-inch pie pan bottom and sides with vegetable cooking spray. Beat egg white at high speed, gradually adding sugar. Beat until sugar dissolves and stiff peaks form. Fold in macadamia nut bits. Spread mixture on bottom and sides of prepared pie pan. Bake at 400° for 12 minutes or until crust is lightly browned. Cool. Crush candy bars with knife blade in food processor or blender. Soften 2 cups of macadamia ice cream in microwave at High 5 seconds. Spread the softened ice cream into cooled crust. Sprinkle with half the crushed candy bars. Freeze. Repeat procedure with remaining ice cream and crushed candy bars. Freeze until firm. Stand at room temperature 5 minutes before serving.

Macadamia Tea Balls

Yield: 3 dozen

1/4 cup butter

1/2 cup sifted powdered sugar

1/4 cup sour cream

2 teaspoons vanilla flavoring

1 1/4 cups all-purpose flour

1/3 cup macadamia nut bits

Cream butter with 6 tablespoons powdered sugar. Beat at medium speed of electric mixer until mixture is light and fluffy. Add sour cream and vanilla and beat. Stir in flour and macadamia nut bits. Form dough into a ball, wrap in foil, and chill 1 hour or overnight. Lightly coat a cookie sheet with vegetable cooking spray. Roll one-inch dough pieces between palms, forming tea ball cookies. Space cookies two inches apart on prepared cookie sheet. Bake at 350° for 14 minutes or until cookies are lightly browned. Cool on wire rack. Sift remaining powdered sugar over cookies before they are completely cool. These easy-to-make cookies are wonderfully rich. They can be frozen for up to 6 months.

Macadamia Crispers

Yield: 1 dozen

1/4 cup finely chopped macadamia nut bits

1/4 cup sugar

1 egg white

1 tablespoon melted butter

1 tablespoon all-purpose flour

1/2 teaspoon ground cinnamon

Mix all ingredients. Generously coat a cookie sheet with vegetable cooking spray. Make four cookies at a time by spooning 1 1/2 teaspoons of batter into each quarter of prepared cookie sheet. Spread each cookie portion evenly with a metal spatula making a four-inch by three-inch oval. Bake at 425° for 3 minutes or until cookie edges are golden. Cool 20 seconds and then carefully loosen cookies with spatula, but do not remove them from the sheet. Place one cookie upside down on counter and quickly roll it lengthwise around the handle of a wooden spoon. Remove cookie, and let it cool on wire rack. Repeat procedure with remaining cookies as quickly as possible. Should cookies get stiff, return to oven briefly to soften them. Continue procedure with remaining batter. These cookies look terrific on top of a scoop of ice cream or sorbet.

Macadamia Holiday Stuffing

Yield: approximately 6 cups

3/4 cup margarine

1 1/2 cups chopped onion

1 1/2 cups chopped celery with leaves

1/4 cup chopped parsley

8 cups whole-wheat breadcrumbs

1/2 cup sherry

1 egg, beaten

2 tablespoons poultry seasoning

1 cup macadamia nut bits

2 tablespoons orange zest

Place first four ingredients into 2-quart glass measure and microwave at High 5 minutes or sauté on stove top. Add remaining ingredients and mix. Stuff fowl.

Macadamia Salad Dressing

Yield: approximately 2 cups

½   cup macadamia nut bits

½   teaspoon tarragon

½   teaspoon lemon zest

½   teaspoon nutmeg

1   cup macadamia oil

⅓   cup vinegar

Optional: Add 1 teaspoon honey for a
   sweet fruit dressing.

Blend all ingredients and mix well before using. Use this salad dressing for both a green or fruit salad. It is especially good on a spinach salad. Allow 2 tablespoons of salad dressing for each cup of greens.

Macadamia Chicken

Yield: 4 servings

1   cup macadamia nut bits

1   cup corn flake crumbs

1   teaspoon paprika

½   teaspoon onion powder

½   teaspoon ground oregano

½   teaspoon dry mustard

½   cup evaporated skimmed milk

2   pounds skinless chicken thighs

Lightly coat a baking dish with vegetable cooking spray. Combine nuts and the next five ingredients in a shallow bowl. Pour milk into a second shallow bowl. Dip each chicken thigh into milk and dredge it in the nut mixture. Place chicken in prepared baking dish and bake uncovered at 350° for 1 hour or until done. This easy-to-prepare entrée makes a nice family dinner yet is special enough for company.

Mango

Mangifera indica

GROWN IN INDIA for at least 4,000 years, perhaps 6,000 years, mango is one of the earliest cultivated fruits. A grove of mangos was given to Buddha for meditation. In the sixteenth century, the Mogul emperor Akbar the Great loved mango so much that he planted a vast orchard of 100,000 mango trees near Darbhanga in northeastern India. The name of the fruit was westernized by the Portuguese, India's trading partner, to mango from the Tamil word *man-kay*.

Mango is described as the world's most delicious fruit, the "king of fruits." In many parts of the world, mango consumption exceeds that of apple and in the worldwide production of fruit, mango ranks fifth. Asia accounts for three-fourths of the mango production; India, which has more than 500 commercial varieties, is the main producer. Mexico and Pakistan follow India in mango production. Mango grows in most subtropical places—the Caribbean, Africa, South America, the Philippines, Australia, Florida, California, and Hawai'i.

Mango plants, brought to Hawai'i from Manila about 1824, were given to Don Francisco de Paula Marin, Spanish horticulturist. He was known to the Hawaiians as "Manini," and his first mango tree was called "manini" mango. Mango plants were imported to Hawai'i from Jamaica in 1885, and 14 years later S. M. Damon brought the Pirie from India to Moanalua Gardens. The first Hawai'i Territorial Mango Forum in 1955 honored David T. Fleming, who introduced the Haden mango on Maui.

The mango tree is a deep-rooted, symmetrical evergreen that can grow to ninety feet, be eighty feet wide, and bear fruit for 40 years. In Hawai'i, mangos grow from sea level to 1,500 feet, but are most productive below 1,200 feet. Hawaiian mangos prefer a hot, dry area with little wind. Trees normally bear at 3–5 years, with maximum production occurring after 15–20 years.

Mango leaves are about thirteen inches long, limp, and deep red, turning a deep, glossy green when mature. The tree is resinous throughout, with the gum and bark used medicinally as an astringent. The leaves, sap, and bark may cause a rash for some people.

The one-fourth-inch pale, pink-white flowers bloom at various times from December to April. Fruit appears 3–5 months after flowering. The harvest season in Hawai'i is normally June–September, but mangos can usually be found somewhere in the Islands anytime. For the past 60 years, the mango harvest of "summer" large and "winter" small appears to be merging.

Many recognized varieties of mangos, as well as unnamed hybrids, are grown in Hawai'i. Mangos come in many shapes—oval, round, oblong, and even banana-shaped. Fruit color varies from green to yellow-orange and even burgundy. The flesh can be pale yellow to orange, smooth, or fibrous and adheres to a fuzzy, striated flat seed. Most mangos in Hawai'i weigh from one-fourth to three pounds, are six inches long, and have a smooth, one-eighth-inch-thick skin; but the many varieties of mango can be quite dissimilar.

The enticing aroma of a mango intensifies its flavor. The fruit's aroma, texture, and taste have been cultivated and improved by generations of gardeners. The differences in taste among mango varieties reflect a combination of sweetness, acidity, and aroma. Some authorities believe that changes in the diurnal temperature at ripening time account for better taste.

Use

Mangos bruise easily and should be picked when mature but not ripe. When buying mangos, select unripe, firm fruit and ripen at room temperature. Unripe mangos can be kept refrigerated for 2–3 weeks. Ripe mango is firm but not hard, shows color in the skin, and has deep yellow to orange flesh.

A mango connoisseur knows the right way to eat a ripe mango— over the kitchen sink with juice to the elbow. If served an unpeeled mango, "hedgehog" it. This Australian technique involves cutting off both puffy cheeks and making cross-cuts through the flesh, not the skin. Then, flex the cheek to convex and remove the flesh.

Use ripe mangos in smoothies, ice cream, jam, bread, and salad. Mango combines well with most fruits and vegetables, meat, poultry, and even seafood. No appreciable amount of vitamin content is lost during cooking or freezing.

Green, mature mango has pale green to light yellow flesh and does not yield to the touch. The taste of green mango is reminiscent of an unripe, tart apple. A local favorite in Hawai'i is green mango eaten with equal parts of vinegar and soy sauce and, perhaps, salt and pepper. Green mango can be shredded in a food processor, sliced, or puréed. Chutney is the most common use for green mango but it is also good in soup, relish, sauce, jam, and curry.

Green, immature mango differs from green, mature mango both in the smaller size and in the softness of the seed. In Hawai'i, the immature fruit is usually pickled. The mangos are peeled and then the seed kernel is sliced through and removed. In some parts of the world, the mango is pickled unpeeled, thus retaining valuable vitamins.

Candied or dehydrated mango can be purchased or can be prepared at home. Use for snacks, cookies or cakes, and toppings.

Ripe and green purée, shredded mango, and mango slices freeze well. Peel and freeze mango plain rather than in a simple syrup to increase its versatility. It is not necessary to defrost a whole package of mango as portions can be sliced off with a sharp knife and the remainder returned to the freezer. Optimal storage time for frozen mango is 9 months.

Mango Chutney

Yield: approximately 4 quarts

Chutney flavor and texture are matters of choice. The size of the fruit pieces can vary from one-half inch to as large as two inches. Chutney thickens only slightly when cooled, so it should be cooked to the desired consistency. Chutney can be cooked entirely on the stove, where it must be carefully watched to prevent sticking or burning. It can also be finished in the microwave in small batches where it needs no stirring and will not burn. The cooking time is reduced if part of the recipe is finished on the stove and part is finished in the microwave.

This basic chutney recipe can be used with a wide variety of fruits and can be adapted for a sweeter or milder chutney by increasing or decreasing the proportions of chili peppers, sugar, and fruit.

3   cups white vinegar

3   pounds granulated sugar

12 cups chopped green mango

4   teaspoons salt

2   teaspoons nutmeg

2   teaspoons ground cloves

2   teaspoons allspice

2   teaspoons ground ginger

1   teaspoon mace

1   teaspoon cinnamon

1/2 cup orange zest

3   cups currants

4   onions, chopped

6   tiny red chilies, deseeded and crushed

2   tablespoons mustard seeds

5   garlic cloves, crushed

1/2 cup chopped fresh gingerroot

Optional: 1/2 pound slivered almonds.

Boil vinegar and sugar in a large pan for 5 minutes to dissolve sugar. Add all other ingredients. Simmer and stir constantly to mix well. The chutney can be cooked to desired consistency over low heat on the stove or finished in the microwave. Pour or spoon into sterilized jars or freezer bags. Chutney can be refrigerated or frozen for up to 6 months.

Microwave method: Place 4 cups of the mixture into a 2-quart pourable glass measure. Microwave at High to desired consistency about 15 minutes. Repeat procedure for remaining ingredients.

Fast Mango Holiday Chutney

Yield: 5 cups

Use either fresh or frozen green or ripe mango for this colorful and spicy chutney.

1   cup apricot jam

1   cup water

1   teaspoon curry powder

1   teaspoon ground ginger

1   teaspoon ground cinnamon

4   whole cloves

1   unpeeled, finely minced lime

2   cups chopped mango

1   hard pear, diced

2   cups fresh cranberries

½   cup golden raisins or currants

Combine first six ingredients in large saucepan over medium heat. Stir and bring to boil. Add lime, mango, and pear. Cook 3 minutes. Add cranberries and raisins and cook 10 minutes. Cool to room temperature but chill before serving. Serve with poultry and pork.

Green Mango-Cucumber Relish

Yield: 4 cups

¾   cup cider vinegar

2   tablespoons brown sugar

½   teaspoon celery seeds

2   tablespoons minced fresh mint

¼   teaspoon white pepper

2   cucumbers, unpeeled and thinly sliced

2   cups thinly sliced or shredded green mango

Mix first five ingredients in a small bowl until brown sugar dissolves. Mix cucumber and mango in a 2-quart container. Pour dressing over cucumber and mango. Cover and chill at least 4 hours. Drain and discard liquid before serving.

Pickled Mango

Yield: 4 quarts

16 cups mango chunks

3 cups water

2 cups cider vinegar

2½ cups brown sugar

¼ cup Hawaiian or kosher salt, to taste

1 tablespoon Chinese five spice

⅓ pound seedless li hing mui (preserved plum), to taste

1 teaspoon mace

2 tablespoons chopped fresh gingerroot

Use immature mango that can be cut through the seed. Peel and remove seed husks or kernels. Cut mango into pickle-size chunks. Place mango chunks into sterilized jars. Place remaining ingredients in large saucepan over medium heat. Bring to a boil and cook 5 minutes while stirring to dissolve brown sugar. Pour pickle syrup over mangos and seal jars immediately. Cool at room temperature but keep refrigerated.

Mango Salsa

Yield: 3 cups

2 cups shredded green mango or green papaya

1 cup slightly mashed avocado

3 tablespoons lime juice

½ cup diced green onion

2 garlic cloves, minced

1 teaspoon black pepper

1 teaspoon coriander seeds

1 teaspoon minced Chinese parsley (cilantro)

Optional: Bottled chili pepper sauce to taste.

Combine all ingredients. Flavors blend when refrigerated 2 hours or overnight. Serve with beef, poultry, seafood, or Mexican food.

Cheese and Chutney

1   (15-ounce) mini-Brie cheese
½   cup mango chutney

Remove a circle of rind from top of cheese, leaving one-half-inch rim of rind. Spread chutney over top of cheese. Microwave cheese and chutney at High 2 minutes. Serve with crackers, pineapple spears, or carambola stars.

Alternate method: Warm cheese and chutney for 5 minutes at 300°.

Traditional Cheese and Chutney   Yield: 8 servings

1   (8-ounce) package cream cheese
1   cup mango chutney

Place cream cheese on serving dish and cover with chutney. Surround platter with crackers or rye bread.

Scallops in Mango Sauce   Yield: 4 servings

1   teaspoon dried tarragon leaves
1   teaspoon dried basil
2   tablespoons chopped fresh parsley
1½ cups clam juice
½   teaspoon ground pepper
1½ pounds scallops
4   ounces spinach fettuccine, uncooked
1   cup mango juice (about 3 mangos)
1   cup plain yogurt
1   (3-ounce) package low-fat cream cheese, softened

Combine first 5 ingredients in a saucepan and bring to a boil. Reduce heat and simmer 3 minutes. Add scallops and cook 5 minutes or until scallops are opaque. Drain scallops and discard liquid. Cook fettuccine according to package directions. Drain. Transfer fettuccine to a serving platter; top with scallops. Barely warm mango juice at low heat, blend in yogurt and softened cream cheese. Spoon sauce over scallops.

Mango Tabbouleh

This variation of a classic Middle Eastern dish is a clean-tasting salad using cracked wheat and mango or pineapple. It can be eaten with a fork, but is fun to scoop up with a piece of romaine lettuce.

2 cups passion fruit juice or pine-apple juice

1 cup bulgur (cracked wheat)

$1/2$ cup cooked brown rice

$1/2$ cup olive oil

$1/4$ cup lemon juice

$1/2$ teaspoon cumin

$1/2$ teaspoon turmeric

$1/2$ teaspoon coriander seeds

$1/3$ cup finely chopped, fresh mint

8 minced green onions

1 cup minced, fresh parsley

2 cups diced firm mango, drained or 2 cups fresh pineapple chunks, drained

Garnish: $1/2$ cup pomegranate seeds.

Bring fruit juice and bulgur to boil in covered pan. Reduce heat and simmer for 5 minutes. Bulgur should remain crunchy and water should be absorbed. Place bulgur, rice, and the next five ingredients into a large bowl. Toss. Add remaining ingredients and mix thoroughly. Cover and chill at least 1 hour. To serve, line a platter with romaine leaves and pile fruited tabbouleh in center.

Garnish with pomegranate seeds.

Chutney Salad Dressing

Yield: 2 cups

The practical and tasty reason for using chutney in salad dressings, marinades, and sauces is that it contains garlic, onion, ginger, and chilies, which makes it unnecessary to add additional seasonings. This dressing goes equally well with fruit, seafood, meat, and poultry salad.

1 cup mango chutney

¼ cup low-cholesterol mayonnaise

½ cup plain low-fat yogurt

Combine all ingredients.

Mango Fruit Spread

Yield: 4 cups

2½ cups drained 1-inch mango chunks

1½ cups drained 1-inch pineapple chunks

2 tablespoons lemon zest

1 package fruit pectin for light jam

2 teaspoons ground cinnamon

1 teaspoon ground cloves

Optional: Honey to taste.

Place all ingredients into a 3- to 4-quart saucepan over medium heat. Stir to dissolve and boil 1 minute while stirring constantly. Remove fruit spread from heat. Pour into sterilized containers or freezer bags. Cool at room temperature 24 hours and then freeze up to 6 months or refrigerate up to 3 months. Do not store at room temperature. This spreadable fruit tastes fresh and has a lovely color and texture.

Mango-Chocolate Fruit Spread

Yield: 2 cups

2 cups mango fruit spread

3 tablespoons almond- or orange-flavored liqueur

½ cup finely chopped semisweet chocolate morsels

Chop chocolate morsels in food processor until fine. Mix all ingredients and pour into sterilized container. Keep refrigerated. The chocolate melts when spread on hot toast or muffins. This unusual spread is an attractive gift.

Rock Cornish Game Hen

Yield: 4 servings

These delicious game hens are easy to prepare and can be eaten hot or cold. The basting sauce is also good on beef kabobs or ribs. If the menu is a simple one, allow a whole bird per person, but if several items will be served, half a game hen is sufficient. Game hens are good grilled, oven roasted, or cooked in the microwave.

2 game hens split lengthwise

Sauce:

½ cup low-sodium soy sauce

½ cup catsup

¼ cup mango chutney

Garnish: Watercress sprigs

Mix sauce ingredients in a small bowl. Arrange game hens in a microwave-safe baking dish with thickest portions toward outside. Cover and microwave at High 10 minutes. Drain. Brush hens with sauce. Cover and microwave at High 5 minutes. Rearrange hens and brush with sauce. Microwave an additional 5 minutes or until hens are done. Let stand covered 3 minutes before serving. Garnish with watercress.

Oven method: Arrange game hens in baking dish and spoon one-half sauce mixture over them. Cover and roast at 350° 30 minutes. Uncover hens and spoon remaining sauce over them. Roast uncovered until done, about 10 minutes. Remove to serving platter.

Just-for-Fun Tropical Doughnuts Yield: 2 dozen

Homemade doughnuts have a marvelous flavor unavailable in a commercial product. Nothing matches the taste of a freshly baked homemade bread product. Doughnuts can be frozen up to 3 months and reheated in the microwave or in the oven with good results. For toppings, shake doughnuts in a mixture of cinnamon and sugar while warm, or glaze with a chocolate, vanilla, or fruit icing.

3   tablespoons butter

1/2 cup sugar

2   eggs

1/4 cup milk

1 1/2 cups mashed and drained mango, pineapple, or banana

5   cups flour

1 1/2 tablespoons baking powder

1/2 teaspoon salt

1   teaspoon nutmeg

1   teaspoon cinnamon

Additional flour as needed for cutting surface, hands, and proper dough consistency

About 4 cups (2 inches) vegetable oil heated to 375° in deep skillet or wok

Cinnamon topping:

1   cup granulated sugar

1   tablespoon cinnamon

Fruit glaze topping:

2   cups confectioners' sugar

1/3 cup strained fruit juice (use mango, guava, lemon, orange, passion fruit, pineapple)

Cream butter and sugar in large bowl. Add eggs. Beat well. Stir in milk and mashed fruit. Combine flour, baking powder, salt, nutmeg, and cinnamon in separate bowl. Add half the flour mixture to fruit mixture. Mix. Add remaining flour mixture to the fruit mixture and mix well. Place dough onto floured surface. Knead lightly with well-floured hands, using additional flour if needed. Roll or pat dough to one-half inch thickness. Cut with floured 2 1/2-inch doughnut cutter. Knead scraps of dough together to make additional doughnuts. Drop three or four doughnuts at a time into the hot oil. Cook 1 minute per side or until brown. Drain. Place a few hot doughnuts at a time into a bag with cinnamon topping ingredients and shake to coat or dip warm doughnut tops in fruit glaze and let them dry on a rack 5 minutes.

To make fruit glaze topping: Whisk sugar and fruit juice until smooth.

Mango Chutney Biscuits

Yield: 1 dozen

1½ cups all-purpose flour

1 tablespoon baking powder

¼ teaspoon baking soda

1 tablespoon sugar

3 tablespoons margarine

2 egg whites, lightly beaten

½ cup mango chutney

2 tablespoons orange zest

Coat a baking sheet with vegetable cooking spray. Combine flour, baking powder, baking soda, and sugar. Cut in margarine to resemble coarse meal. In a separate bowl, combine egg whites, chutney, and orange zest. Add egg mixture to flour mixture. Stir to moisten dry ingredients. Drop by tablespoonfuls onto prepared baking sheet. Bake at 400° for 15 minutes. These biscuits are the perfect accompaniment to a soup or salad course.

Mango Nut Treat Bread

Yield: 1 loaf

1½ cups ½-inch mango pieces

1¼ cups all-purpose flour

¼ cup granulated sugar

¼ cup brown sugar

1½ teaspoons baking powder

¼ teaspoon baking soda

¼ teaspoon salt

1 teaspoon ground cloves

1 teaspoon ground cinnamon

1 teaspoon ground nutmeg

1 egg, beaten

½ cup strawberry, papaya, or plain yogurt

¼ cup vegetable oil

2 teaspoons almond flavoring

4 tablespoons macadamia nut or peanut bits

4 tablespoons butterscotch morsels

Lightly coat 9 by 5 by 3-inch pan with vegetable cooking spray. Drain mango pieces in salad spinner or drain and pat with paper towel to remove excess juice. Combine the next nine ingredients in a large bowl. Combine egg, yogurt, oil, almond flavoring, and 2 tablespoons of the nut bits. Add yogurt mixture to dry ingredients. Fold in drained mango pieces. Spoon batter into prepared pan.

Combine remaining 2 tablespoons of nut bits with butterscotch morsels. Sprinkle over batter. Bake at 350° for 55 minutes or until done. Cool in pan 10 minutes. Remove from pan and cool on wire rack. Wrap bread in foil and refrigerate 8 hours to enhance flavor.

This richly flavored bread makes an attractive gift when wrapped with tinted cellophane and ribbon or wrapped and placed into a wicker basket.

Mango in Chocolate Cups

Yield: 8 servings

This dessert is simple and elegant. It can be prepared ahead by removing foil from frozen chocolate shells and returning them to the freezer. Shells can be filled quickly with the refrigerated mango mixture and garnished.

8	2 by 1-inch foil baking cups lightly coated with vegetable cooking spray
4	1-ounce squares semisweet chocolate
2	tablespoons crème de menthe or favorite liqueur
2	cups chopped firm mango, papaya, or lychee halves

Garnish: 8 small mint sprigs

Microwave chocolate in 2-cup glass measure at Medium Low 2–3 minutes. Stir. Using a metal spoon, spread melted chocolate evenly one-eighth inch thick on bottom and sides of prepared baking cups. Freeze about 1 hour. Mix liqueur and mango and refrigerate 1 hour.

To serve: Remove chocolate shells from foil cups, working quickly but gently while chocolate is frozen. Fill shells with mango mixture. Garnish with mint before serving.

Mango Chutney Ice Cream

Yield: 4 servings

1	quart vanilla ice cream, softened
1	cup mango chutney

Mix chutney into softened ice cream and freeze. This creamy, uniquely flavored ice cream is good alone or as an ice cream pie with a chocolate cookie crust.

Papaya

Carica papaya

ONCE USED IN the Islands for chicken and pig food, the papaya is now a favorite on most menus. Each day, more mainland consumers discover this Island delicacy. Papaya is the major fruit crop of the Big Island and the second major fruit crop in Hawai'i after pineapple.

How and when papaya became established in Hawai'i is a mystery. Historical journals note it as growing in Don Francisco de Paula Marin's gardens in 1831. Papaya is a New World fruit native to South and Central America. The name "papaya" is a Spanish adaptation of *ababai*, from the pre-Columbian people in the Caribbean. Papaya should not be confused with papaw, the American custard apple, even though papaw is used in Australia to mean papaya.

Papaya looks like a melon, but grows on a tree (actually, a large, hollow, unbranched herbaceous shrub). It grows wild in many gulches on all Islands where seeds have been spread by birds, animals, and humans. The papaya plant can grow to thirty feet, but the University of Hawai'i recently developed five- to six-foot varieties that make picking easier. Trees bear in their first year, with the best crops in the second to fourth year. In commercial operations, fields are usually abandoned or replanted after three years.

The papaya fruits cluster along the plant stem under a crown of leaves. The one-inch flowers are creamy white, fragrant, and can be used for leis.

Because papaya dates from prehistoric times, it has proliferated into dozens of horticultural varieties. Some fruits are tiny and others are as large as watermelons. Papaya can be a one-inch fruit with lots of seeds or a thick-fleshed fruit twenty inches long weighing fifteen pounds. Most market-size papaya weigh 1¼ pounds, are six to twelve inches long, and have five shallow grooves from top to bottom. The flesh is yellow-green to deep orange, with green, smooth skin turning yellow when ripe. A cavity in the center of the fruit is filled with numerous small, round, shiny, black seeds that have a peppery taste.

Use

Green, firm, unbruised papaya ripens at room temperature in 3–5 days, and ripe papaya can be refrigerated for a week. Because papaya lacks acidity, the addition of lime or lemon improves and intensifies the fruit's flavor. To serve papaya, halve it, remove one-half inch of the stem end, and scoop out the seeds, which can be saved and pulverized for salad dressings or marinade. Fruit can also be peeled and cut into rings for salads or entrées. Ripe papaya makes good sauce, marinade, ice cream, smoothies, and bread. Green papaya is used in soups and stews, and as a vegetable—stuffed, boiled, or baked. The cool, bland fruit goes well with spicy foods.

Papain, a beneficial enzyme in papaya believed to aid digestion, makes papaya a practical dessert choice. Because it is a meat tenderizer, puréed papaya is an excellent addition to marinades. Even the papaya leaf wrapped around meat will tenderize it.

Uncooked papaya, like uncooked pineapple and kiwi, will not congeal in commercial gelatin that has a protein (animal) base. It can be used with agar, a seaweed base. Use a commercial pectin, or other fruits that have abundant pectin, when making papaya jam or chutney.

Peeled, firm papaya can be frozen in chunks or as a purée. Do not use overripe fruit. The frozen fruit is suitable for dessert or entrée sauce, baking, soup, salad dressing, and marinade.

Papaya Appetizer Logs

Yield: approximately 20 servings

2   (8-ounce) packages low-fat cream cheese, softened

1   cup low-fat cottage cheese

1   tablespoon curry powder

1   cup minced green onions

3/4   cup papaya or other fruit chutney

Combine cream cheese, cottage cheese, and curry powder in a food processor container. Process until smooth using metal blade. Add green onions and stir in the chutney. Cover and chill 20 minutes. Divide mixture in half and shape each portion into a twelve-inch log. Wrap in wax paper and chill at least 6 hours or until logs are firm. Place logs onto a serving tray. Serve with whole-grain crackers.

Variation: Press 1/4 cup coarsely chopped macadamia nuts onto the top and sides of the chilled logs.

Tip: To soften cream cheese, microwave at Medium 30 seconds.

Easy Party Appetizer

Keep meatballs, Vienna sausages, or hot dog cubes bubbling hot in a chafing dish and offer guests a choice of papaya salsa or papaya-peanut dip.

Pacific-Style Stuffed Fishcake   Yield: 20 servings

This fishcake is broiled around a rod, making a hollow center for fillings. The outside of the cream-colored fishcake is nicely browned.

2   chikuwa fishcake

1   (8-ounce) package low-fat cream cheese, softened

½   cup coarsely chopped shrimp, crab, or clam

½   cup papaya, mango, or avocado purée

¼   cup minced green onion

¼   cup minced fresh spinach or watercress

2   tablespoons low-cholesterol mayonnaise

2   tablespoons soy sauce

Garnish: Chinese parsley (cilantro) sprigs

Slit one side of fishcake lengthwise to facilitate stuffing. Thoroughly blend stuffing ingredients in large bowl. Stuff fishcake. Bring cut sides together and place cut side down. Wrap fishcake and chill at least 2 hours. Slice stuffed fishcake into appetizer portions and garnish.

Warm Chunky Papaya-Peanut Dip   Yield: 2 cups

2   (6-ounce) cartons papaya or lemon yogurt

1   cup no-sugar-added chunky peanut butter

1   cup ¼-inch papaya chunks

Blend all ingredients and warm in microwave at High 3 minutes.

Alternate method: Place all ingredients into medium saucepan and warm over low heat, stirring constantly, 3–5 minutes. Serve warm.

Papaya Salsa

Yield: 3 cups

2 large tomatoes

1 medium-sized purple onion

1 jalapeño pepper or to taste

1 garlic clove

3 tablespoons red wine vinegar

1/2 teaspoon ground cumin

1 teaspoon coriander seeds

2 cups shredded or finely chopped green papaya

1 tablespoon minced Chinese parsley (cilantro)

Cut tomatoes and onion into suitable sizes for food processor. Position metal blade in processor bowl and add all ingredients except coriander seeds, parsley, and papaya. Cover and pulse five or six times until mixture is chunky. Remove to medium bowl, add coriander seeds, parsley, and papaya, cover, and chill at least 3 hours before serving.

Papaya-Citrus Marinade

Yield: 2 cups

The papain enzyme in papaya makes this fruit especially suitable for tenderizing meat in marinades. Use this zippy marinade for beef or poultry.

1 cup papaya purée

1 tablespoon lime zest

1/3 cup grapefruit juice

1/2 cup low-sodium soy sauce

1 tablespoon honey

1/2 teaspoon red pepper flakes

1 tablespoon coarse black pepper

1/2 teaspoon basil leaves

2 tablespoons olive oil

Combine and mix all ingredients except olive oil. Gradually add olive oil and mix. Boil marinade after removing the marinated food and before basting during cooking.

Papaya-Chicken Rice Soup

Yield: 4 servings

4 medium-sized firm, ripe papayas

2 cans condensed chicken and rice soup

1 can water

1/4 cup minced sweet red or green bell pepper

1/2 teaspoon gingerroot juice

A papaya makes a colorful and unusual soup tureen. If necessary, trim a small amount from the bottom of the papaya so that it stands vertically. Cut down two inches from the top of the papaya and save the top. Remove seeds and pulp, leaving one-fourth inch of flesh on the shell. Reserve seeds for salad dressing or another use. Purée the papaya pulp and transfer it to a medium saucepan. Add soup, water, diced bell pepper, and gingerroot juice. Heat to serving temperature and fill papayas two-thirds full. Replace tops before serving. Two filled papayas can be warmed in the microwave at High for 3 minutes.

Variation: Use condensed golden mushroom soup.

Papaya Salad Dressing

Yield: 2 cups

1/2 cup low-cholesterol mayonnaise

1/2 cup plain low-fat yogurt

1/2 cup papaya chunks

1/4 teaspoon ground cloves

1 tablespoon curry powder

2 tablespoons dark rum or orange juice

Combine all ingredients in container bowl of blender or food processor and mix to desired consistency. Refrigerate several hours before serving. This creamy dressing is particularly good with a molded fruit or vegetable salad.

Papaya Seed Dressing

Yield: 2 cups

The peppery taste of crushed papaya seeds adds texture and a piquant flavor to a traditional vinegar-and-oil salad dressing. Use it on greens, a fruit salad, or as a marinade. Papaya seeds can be crushed in the food processor using a metal blade or in a blender. The excess crushed seeds can be refrigerated with a small amount of oil for 2 weeks. If adding crushed papaya seeds to a purchased oil-and-vinegar salad dressing, allow 2 tablespoons of crushed seeds to 8 ounces of dressing.

4   tablespoons crushed papaya seeds

2   tablespoons fresh rosemary or
     2 teaspoons dried rosemary

1   tablespoon fresh tarragon or
     1 teaspoon dried tarragon

1   minced garlic clove

1   tablespoon lime zest, lemon zest,
     or passion fruit pulp

1/3   cup red wine vinegar or to taste

2   cups salad oil, olive oil, or macadamia nut oil

Place all ingredients except oil into a large mixing bowl and stir to moisten. Use a wire whisk to combine the oil with the dressing ingredients. Chill at least 1 hour before serving.

Green Papaya Relish

Yield: 2 cups

1   large green papaya

1   tablespoon lime juice

1   tablespoon coriander seeds

Salt and coarse black pepper to taste

1   minced mild chili pepper

Peel and deseed papaya. Use the food processor cheese shredder attachment to shred papaya. Combine all ingredients and chill before serving. This pale green relish complements fish and seafood.

Papaya Chutney

Yield: approximately 6 pints

Chutney thickens only slightly when cooled, so it should be cooked to the desired consistency. Chutney can be cooked entirely on the stove, where it must be carefully watched to prevent sticking and burning. Or it can be finished in smaller amounts in the microwave, where it needs little stirring and does not readily burn. Cooking time is reduced if a portion of the chutney is finished on the stove and the remainder is finished in the microwave. This recipe works with slightly more or slightly less papaya.

10 cups 1-inch green papaya chunks

3 cups cider vinegar

1/2 cup honey

2 teaspoons ground cloves

2 teaspoons allspice

1 teaspoon mace

2 tablespoons paprika

2 tablespoons lime zest

3 tablespoons horseradish

2 tablespoons mustard seeds

2 tablespoons celery seeds

1/4 cup finely chopped fresh ginger-root

2 (4-ounce) jars diced pimento, drained

Peel and deseed papaya and cut into 1-inch chunks. Bring vinegar and honey to a boil in a large pan, stirring constantly. Add remaining ingredients. Simmer and stir to mix well. The chutney can be cooked to desired consistency over low heat or finished in the microwave. Pour or spoon into sterilized jars or freezer bags. Cool chutney at room temperature. Refrigerate the chutney 1 month or freeze 3 months. This robust chutney is good with turkey or beef and excellent on ham or chicken sandwiches.

Microwave method: Place 4 cups of the chutney mixture into a 2-quart pourable glass measure. Microwave at High to desired consistency, stirring every 3 minutes. Repeat procedure for remaining ingredients.

Papaya Catsup

Yield: 6 cups

This colorful condiment is excellent on chicken sandwiches. Papaya catsup can substitute for vinegar in an oil-and-vinegar salad dressing. This recipe works with either papaya, mango, or a combination of the two fruits.

5	tablespoons pickling spice
2	tablespoons chopped gingerroot
3	cloves garlic
1	red onion
2	small chilies or to taste
6	cups papaya or mango purée
1	(8-ounce) can pineapple tidbits, undrained
1	cup vinegar
1/4	cup brown sugar
2	tablespoons paprika
1	tablespoon ground allspice
3	tablespoons mustard seeds

Zest from 1 lime

Place first five ingredients in food processor or blender container and use knife blade to finely chop ingredients. Place purée in large pan and combine all ingredients. Cook over medium heat for about 20 minutes, stirring frequently to avoid sticking. Pour into hot, sterilized jars. Seal, cool, and refrigerate 2 weeks. Fruit catsup can be frozen in freezer bags for up to 3 months.

Microwave method: Combine and mix all ingredients with fruit purée. Place 4 cups of the mixture into a 2-quart pourable glass measure. Microwave at High 10 minutes or until thick. Repeat procedure for remaining ingredients.

Papaya Butter

Yield: 4 cups

The flavor of this smooth tropical spread is enhanced with minced lime. It is best cooked in the microwave to avoid scorching. Good with English muffins, bagels, biscuits, and pancakes.

4	cups papaya purée
1/4	cup guava juice
1	lime, unpeeled and minced
1	cinnamon stick or 1 tablespoon ground cinnamon
1	tablespoon allspice

Optional: Honey to taste.

Combine all ingredients in a 2-quart glass measure. Microwave at High 5 minutes. Stir. Cook until mixture thickens. Taste and sweeten with honey if desired. Place in sterilized jars or freezer bags. Cool completely and refrigerate up to 3 weeks or freeze up to 3 months. Do not store at room temperature.

Papaya Dessert Sauce

Yield: 2 cups

The use of freshly grated nutmeg instead of ground nutmeg makes a vast difference in the taste and texture of any dish. This simple topping is good with crêpes, raspberry sherbet, and chocolate pound cake.

1 cup papaya purée	Microwave papaya purée at High 2 minutes or warm on stove top. Do not boil. Blend in remaining ingredients. Best served warm.
1 cup ½-inch banana chunks	
1 teaspoon ground nutmeg	
1 teaspoon ground cinnamon	

Optional: 2 tablespoons almond-flavored liqueur.

Sweet Maui Girl Papaya Bread

Yield: 1 loaf

1½ cups all-purpose flour

½ cup whole-wheat flour

½ cup wheat germ

½ cup brown sugar

2 teaspoons baking powder

½ teaspoon baking soda

¼ teaspoon salt

1 tablespoon pumpkin pie spice

1 egg, beaten

1 (8-ounce) carton papaya or lemon yogurt

⅓ cup milk

¼ cup vegetable oil

2 teaspoons vanilla extract

2 cups ¼-inch papaya pieces

Topping:

1 (3-ounce) package low-fat cream cheese, softened

2 tablespoons orange zest

3 tablespoons mashed papaya

Coat a 9 by 5 by 3-inch loaf pan with vegetable cooking spray. Combine first eight ingredients in a large bowl and stir. Combine the next five ingredients in a separate bowl. Add these ingredients to the dry ingredients, stirring to moisten. Fold in fruit. Spoon into prepared pan and bake at 350° for 1 hour or until done. Cool in pan 10 minutes. Remove from pan and cool on wire rack. Combine topping ingredients and spread over bread.

Papaya Brunch Muffins

Yield: 12 muffins

1 cup all-purpose flour

1/2 cup cornmeal

2 teaspoons baking powder

1/4 teaspoon salt

1/3 cup Vienna sausage, cooked ham, or hot dog, sliced to 1/4-inch cubes

1/4 cup extra-sharp Cheddar cheese cubes, sliced to 1/4-inch cubes

1/2 cup papaya purée

1/2 cup milk

3 tablespoons vegetable oil

2 eggs, beaten

Coat muffin pans with vegetable cooking spray. Combine flour, cornmeal, baking powder, salt, meat cubes, and cheese cubes in a large bowl. Make a well in center of mixture. Mix remaining ingredients in a small bowl. Add papaya mixture to dry ingredients and stir to moisten. Spoon batter into prepared muffin pans, filling three-fourths full. Bake at 400° for 20–25 minutes or until done. These hearty muffins are a special treat for a luncheon or supper.

Papaya Cookies

Yield: approximately 5 dozen

1/2 cup butter

1/2 cup honey

2 cups whole wheat flour

2 cups rolled oats

2 tablespoon citrus juice

1 cup papaya purée

1 cup chopped dates

1 cup raisins

Combine butter, 1/4 cup of honey, flour, and oats until crumbly. Press half the mixture into a 13 by 9 by 2-inch baking dish that has been lightly coated with vegetable cooking spray. In a saucepan, combine the remaining honey with the citrus juice. Add papaya, dates, and raisins. Cook and stir over low heat for 3 minutes. Cool slightly and then spread over oats mixture in the pan. Finely crumble remaining oats mixture over the top of the batter. Bake in 400° oven for 20 minutes or until done. Cut into 2 by 1-inch cookies when partly cooled.

Tropical Papaya Smoothie

Yield: 4 servings

1 (8-ounce) carton piña colada yogurt or banana yogurt

½ cup chilled guava or passion fruit juice

1 cup skim milk

1 cup frozen papaya purée

1 cup frozen banana chunks

Ice cubes

Optional: Dash of cinnamon.

Combine all ingredients except ice cubes in container of food processor or blender. Mix to a slushy consistency. Add enough ice cubes to make 4 servings and blend to smooth. Serve in chilled glasses.

Chicken Chutney in Papaya

Yield: 4 servings

Papaya serves as an edible bowl and, complemented with a salad, makes a perfect supper.

2 large, half-ripe papayas

2 cups cooked chicken chunks

1 cup cooked brown rice

½ cup papaya chutney

Cut papayas crosswise 1½ inches from top. Remove top and save. Scoop out seeds and refrigerate for use in marinade or salad dressing. Mix chicken chunks, rice, and chutney in medium bowl. Stuff papayas with the mixture and replace top, securing with toothpicks. Place papayas into microwave-safe container and cook at High 7 minutes. Do not overcook; heat through. Let stand 3 minutes before cutting papayas into halves.

Oven method: Follow stuffing directions. Lightly coat roasting pan with vegetable cooking spray. Cook papayas at 350° for 15 minutes. Do not overcook; heat through. Let stand 3 minutes before cutting papayas into halves.

Papaya, Champagne, and Ice

Yield: 6 servings

2   cups bite-size papaya chunks

1/2 cup kirsch or other cherry liqueur

1   quart lemon or raspberry sorbet

1   bottle chilled champagne

Mix fruit and kirsch and chill 30 minutes. Divide fruit and juice among six champagne glasses. Top fruit with sorbet. Just before serving, pour champagne over sorbet and fruit. Serve immediately.

Fast Papaya Desserts

Sprinkle papaya slices with a little brown sugar and 1 1/2 ounces of vodka or gin. Place under oven broiler until fruit is warm and sugar dissolves. Serve warm. This is good as a sherbet topping.

Add 3 cups papaya chunks to a half gallon of softened strawberry ice cream or ice milk. Refreeze before serving. Top serving portions with fresh strawberry slices.

Cut papaya into finger-size pieces, wipe dry, and freeze to crunchy, about 10 minutes. Coat half the slice with chocolate topping, which forms a hard shell on contact with the cold fruit.

Cool on cool—place scoop of peanut butter–chocolate ice cream or mud pie ice cream in a papaya half.

Make a cheese tray with Bel Paese, Port Salut, Gouda, crackers, and papaya slices.

Gingerbread mix and ripe papayas make a fast upsidedown cake. Melt 1/4 cup butter in a baking pan, add 1/3 cup brown sugar, and stir. Arrange papaya chunks or slices in the syrup. Prepare gingerbread according to package instructions and pour batter over papaya. Bake according to package instructions.

Passion Fruit

Passiflora edulis

THE FLAVOR OF PASSION FRUIT suggests a "taste of the tropics," which changes an ordinary dish or beverage to exotic; however, do not expect guests to be overwhelmed with ardor. The fruit's name is a religious one, coming from Spanish missionaries in South America who saw the gorgeous flowers of the vine as signifying the wounds, nails, cross, crown, and halo of the Passion (suffering) of Christ.

This prolific vine, native to the humid tropics of the Amazon, produces beautiful flowers and tart, sweetly fragrant fruits. It grows commercially in Australia, South and Central America, South Africa, and Hawai'i. It is called liliko'i in Hawai'i because the first seeds in the Islands, brought from Australia by Eugene Delemar in 1880, grew in Liliko'i Gulch on Maui.

Passiflora edulis includes both purple and yellow varieties, but the yellow fruit (*P. edulis* forma *flavicarpa*) is more prevalent in Hawai'i. It is planted along fences as an ornamental, but is also found wild in many parts of the Islands from July until Christmas. About the size and shape of a large egg, this exotic fruit has a tough yellow or dark purple shell. The purple, sometimes called red passion fruit, grows at a higher elevation than the yellow fruit. Inside both varieties is a translucent pulp containing small, round, black seeds. This pulp is the edible part of the fruit.

Use

Passion fruit has an enticing, tropical aroma, and a pungent, refreshing taste. Neither the freshness nor the quality of the pulp dissipates through long storage, freezing, or processing.

Collect passion fruit after it falls to the ground because it is not easy to tell when the fruit is ripe and, usually, it is too high to reach.

Select the heaviest, smoothest fruit, but do not discard ripe passion fruit that is wrinkled. The fruit inside remains fresh and juicy despite the dimpled shell. To prepare passion fruit, cut off the top or cut it in half. Scoop out the pulp with a spoon. Or if hiking, cut a hole at the top of the fruit and suck out the succulent juices.

An easy way to separate the seeds from the pulp is to heat the pulp, which loosens the seeds. Then strain, cool, and refrigerate or freeze the pulp and discard the seeds. The pulp can be strained without heating, but it takes longer to separate the pulp and the seeds. It is also possible to purée the pulp, then strain it to remove seeds. Or purée the pulp and don't strain it, using the pulp with the seeds.

Adding a small amount of passion fruit imparts an intense flavor and zip to fruit salads, tropical drinks, sorbet, cakes, sauces, and frostings. The famous Australian dessert Pavlova, named for the Russian ballerina, uses passion fruit. Passion fruit is an ideal punch ingredient and its tartness is perfect for marinade and fruit vinegar. The fruit combines well with orange, pineapple, tangerine, guava, vodka, gin, rum, brandy, and mineral water.

❖❖❖❖❖❖

Passion Fruit Soup

Yield: 4 cups

3   passion fruit

3   cups honeydew melon purée

1/2   cup white wine

1/4   cup lychee juice or pineapple juice

Garnish: 3/4 cup plain yogurt, divided into 3 tablespoons for each soup bowl

Cut passion fruit and scoop out pulp. Purée pulp including seeds. Combine all ingredients and chill. Divide soup among four soup bowls and garnish with yogurt. Serve as a first course or as a dessert with a macaroon.

Fruited Mayonnaise

1/2   cup passion fruit pulp including
      seeds
1   cup low-cholesterol mayonnaise

Blend well. The flavors intensify if refrigerated at least 2 hours. Use as a salad dressing with fruit or chicken salads. Good with meat or poultry sandwiches.

Variation: Add 2 tablespoons spicy mustard.

Paradise Salad Dressing

Yield: 1 1/2 cups

3   passion fruit
2   tablespoons vinegar
1   cup olive oil
2   crushed garlic cloves
1/4   teaspoon cardamom
1   teaspoon paprika
1   teaspoon fresh rosemary

Cut top from passion fruit and scoop out seeds and pulp. Place all ingredients in blender or food processor container and use the steel blade to purée to smooth. Chill at least 30 minutes before using. Can be refrigerated for up to 3 weeks. This unique blend of flavors makes a suitable dressing for fruit, vegetable, or green leaf salads.

Passion Fruit Salsa

Yield: 4 cups

2   passion fruit
2   cups diced tomatoes
1   (4-ounce) can chopped and
      drained green chilies
1/4   cup sliced green olives
1   cup avocado cubes
3   green onions, diced
1/2   teaspoon garlic powder
1   tablespoon olive oil
1   tablespoon red wine vinegar

Cut tops from passion fruit and scoop out pulp and seeds. Mix passion fruit pulp including seeds and remaining ingredients. Flavors blend if refrigerated overnight. Can refrigerate for up to 1 week. Do not freeze. Serve this colorful condiment with Mexican food or steak.

Passion Fruit Spread

Yield: 4 cups

3   passion fruit

1   (12-ounce) can frozen passion fruit–guava concentrate

1   cup mashed papaya

1   teaspoon ground mace

1   teaspoon ground cloves

1   package fruit pectin for light jam

Cut tops from passion fruit. Scoop out seeds and pulp and place into a 3- to 4-quart saucepan over medium heat. Add remaining ingredients and stir to dissolve pectin. Boil 1 minute, stirring constantly. Remove fruit spread from heat. Pour into sterilized containers or freezer bags and cover immediately. Cool at room temperature and freeze up to 6 months or refrigerate for up to 3 months. Do not store at room temperature. Use this tropical spread on English muffins or bagels. It is also good as a filling for layer cakes or warmed as a topping for gingerbread.

Passion Fruit–Lychee Sorbet

Yield: 6 servings

Top this dessert sorbet with cream sherry, a few passion fruit seeds, and lychees for a stunning dessert.

6   passion fruit

1   (20-ounce) can lychees

$2/3$ cup passion fruit juice or orange juice

1   envelope unflavored gelatin

Topping:

$1/2$ cup cream sherry or orange-flavored liqueur

2   teaspoons passion fruit pulp with seeds

3   lychees, halved

Cut top from passion fruit, scoop out pulp and seeds into a 6-cup freezer container. Reserve 2 teaspoons passion fruit pulp for topping. Drain lychees, adding the liquid to a saucepan together with the fruit juice and gelatin. Cut lychees in half, saving six halves for topping. Add remaining lychee halves to freezer container. Cook gelatin mixture over low heat, stirring constantly, until it dissolves. Pour gelatin mixture over fruit. Stir. Cover and freeze until firm, stirring several times during freezing process. To serve, scoop sorbet into chilled stem glasses. Mix cream sherry and remaining fruit in small bowl. Divide topping among portions.

Alternative method: Freeze the mixture in an ice cream freezer according to manufacturer's instructions.

Giant Tofu–Passion Fruit–Guava Smoothie   Yield: 6 servings

½ cup (¼ pound) soft tofu, drained

1 cup skim milk

1½ cups guava nectar

1 cup passion fruit pulp with seeds

Chill all ingredients before mixing for best flavor. Combine tofu and milk in container of an electric blender or food processor and blend 1 minute. Add remaining ingredients and blend. Chill well. This makes a hearty addition to a brunch or breakfast party.

Island Party Punch

Yield: 4 quarts

1 (12-ounce) can frozen passion fruit–guava concentrate

2 cups unsweetened pineapple juice

½ cup passion fruit pulp and seeds

2 cups guava or pineapple purée

3 tablespoons pomegranate syrup

7 cups strong mint tea

3 (28-ounce) bottles ginger ale, chilled

Ice block

Garnish: Citrus zest (orange, lime, or tangerine)

Combine all ingredients except ginger ale and ice. Chill thoroughly. Add mixture to punch bowl and blend well. Add ice block and chilled ginger ale. Garnish.

Variation: Replace ice block and pomegranate syrup with a half gallon of tangerine, lemon, or pineapple sherbet.

Sparkling Mahimahi

Yield: 4 servings

2 pounds mahimahi fillets or fillets from another firm white fish

¼ cup lime juice

1 tablespoon coarse black pepper

1 green onion, sliced

2 tablespoons olive oil

2 tablespoons all-purpose flour

2 cups champagne

½ cup passion fruit pulp and seeds

Garnish: Watercress sprigs

Marinate fish in lime juice at least 15 minutes. Remove fish from marinade, sprinkle with pepper, and broil fillets four inches from heat 6 minutes or until fish flakes easily. Transfer fish onto a serving platter. Sauté onion in olive oil over medium heat. Add flour and stir until smooth. Cook 1 minute. Gradually add champagne, stirring until mixture thickens. Stir in passion fruit and warm. Do not boil. Spoon warm sauce over fish and garnish with watercress.

Persimmon

Diospyros kaki

THIS DECIDUOUS TREE GROWS BEST in a temperate climate well above sea level. Persimmons are native to North America, China, and the Himalayas. In Hawai'i, they are grown commercially in the Kula district of Maui, which is above 2,000-feet elevation. The persimmon flowers in March and April, and the harvest season is October through December.

The round or plum-shaped varieties sold commercially originated in China and Japan and were introduced into the United States shortly after Commodore Perry's expedition to Japan in 1852. This species *(Diospyros kaki)* is now grown in California, Louisiana, Florida, upcountry Maui, Chile, Israel, the Mediterranean area, and North Africa. *Kaki* is the Japanese name for persimmon, and it is used throughout Europe. "Persimmon" is a corruption of the Algonquin Indian name for the fruit.

The persimmon varieties grown in Hawai'i are Fuyu, Maru, and Hachiya. The Fuyu fruit is flat, Maru is round, and Hachiya is heart-shaped and pointed on one end. Persimmons are divided into two main groups: astringent and nonastringent. Astringent types cannot be eaten until fully ripe or they will be bitter. Nonastringent fruit (tannin-free), like the Fuyu, can be eaten at a firmer stage. Both Maru and Hachiya are astringent and need to be fully ripe, soft, and orange. The Fuyu is a lighter orange than the Hachiya when ripe.

Use

Fruit is best picked by clipping the stems to leave the calyx lobes attached to the fruit. To avoid bruising and skin discoloration, handle persimmons carefully. Purchase firm, unblemished fruit; it will ripen at room temperature if sealed in an airtight bag with pieces of apple or with a banana. Persimmon is customarily eaten unpeeled and sliced because the skin is thin. Some varieties have brown seeds that are easy to remove. Serve ripe fruit chilled or partially frozen. If peeling is necessary, remove the stem end first.

Pulp for purée can be scooped with a spoon from the persimmon after stem removal. Use a blender or food processor to purée the pulp. Five or six persimmons will make 1 cup of purée. If freezing purée, allow 1 tablespoon lemon or lime juice for every 2 cups of purée to prevent darkening. Persimmons are good in cakes, puddings, ice cream, frozen yogurt, bread, cookies, sauces, and stuffed for salads or desserts.

Fast Persimmon Tips

❋ Remove pulp from persimmons with shell intact. Mix pulp with turkey, ham, or tuna salad. Fill persimmon shells, chill. Slice stuffed persimmons or serve whole.

❋ Mix equal proportions persimmon purée and plain or fruit-flavored yogurt. Freeze mixture in 8-inch-square pan. For a smooth consistency, process frozen yogurt until fluffy in food processor, but do not thaw. Return yogurt to freezer to harden.

❋ Add bite-size persimmon chunks to salads, puddings, frostings, cottage cheese, ice cream, and cereal.

❋❋❋❋❋❋

Frosty Persimmon Soup

Yield: 4 servings

2 cups persimmon or pineapple purée

1/4 cup passion fruit purée including seeds or 2 tablespoons lime juice

1 (8-ounce) carton piña colada yogurt

1/4 teaspoon ground cloves

2 tablespoons dark rum

Garnish: Dash of cinnamon

Combine all ingredients, except rum and cinnamon, in a medium-sized bowl. Cover and freeze for 30 minutes. Stir in rum, place in individual soup bowls, and garnish. This is the perfect soup for a summer's day or the remembrance of one. Serve slightly slushy as a first course with a small biscuit.

Persimmon Mayonnaise

1/3 cup persimmon or avocado purée

1 cup low-cholesterol mayonnaise

Blend well. Flavors intensify if refrigerated at least 2 hours. This easy-to-make and colorful sandwich spread is good with ham, turkey, and chicken sandwiches as well as with a chicken or a fruit salad.

Persimmon-Sherry Mustard

1/2 cup Dijon-style mustard

1/4 cup persimmon or moya purée

Optional: 2 tablespoons sherry.

Blend well. Flavors intensify if refrigerated at least 2 hours. Use on burgers, hot dogs, and pastrami sandwiches or mix with soy sauce for a dip.

Persimmon Freezer Jam Spread
Yield: 2 cups

2 cups persimmon purée

1 (1³/₄-ounce) package powdered pectin

2 tablespoons brown sugar

1 tablespoon orange juice

2 tablespoons orange zest

1 teaspoon ground cinnamon

1 teaspoon ground nutmeg

Combine all ingredients in medium saucepan over medium heat. Boil 1 minute, stirring constantly. Remove from heat and stir 3 minutes. Spoon into freezer containers or sterilized jars. Cover at once. Let stand at room temperature 24 hours before freezing. Freeze for up to 6 months. Do not store fruit spread at room temperature. Refrigerate. This spicy spread is wonderful on muffins and toast.

Persimmon and Cheese Spread

Cheddar, blue cheese, and cream cheese combine with persimmon for an attractive and unique party appetizer. Serve with whole-grain or plain crackers that will not overpower the delicate flavor of persimmon. The spread is also good as a celery stuffing.

2 cups low-fat cream cheese, softened; or 2 cups Cheddar cheese, shredded; or 2 cups blue cheese, softened	Blend ingredients until creamy. Cover and chill at least 1 hour before serving.
½ cup persimmon purée or ¼ cup passion fruit pulp and seeds	To stuff celery: Wash, trim, and cut celery in three-inch pieces, leaving the leaves intact. Stuff celery, wiping excess filling from celery edges.

Optional: 1 tablespoon port wine.

Frozen Persimmon Dessert I

Ripe persimmon can be frozen up to 3 months. If allowed to thaw completely, the fruit becomes mushy. If eaten partially frozen, persimmon takes on a sherbet-like texture. Serve whole and let guests spoon pulp directly from the skin.

Frozen Persimmon Dessert II   Yield: 4 servings

Cut a hole in four persimmons at the stem end. Scoop out pulp without piercing the skin. Mix pulp with 1 cup chocolate cake or cookie crumbs and ¼ cup kirsch or orange-flavored liqueur. Divide filling equally among persimmon shells and stuff them. Wrap securely and freeze 1 hour or up to 3 months. Serve partially frozen.

Frozen Persimmon Dessert III   Yield: 4 servings

Cut a hole in the fruit at the stem end and remove pulp from four ripe, firm persimmons. Combine pulp with 1 pint softened lemon or tangerine sherbet and 2 tablespoons almond-flavored liqueur or 2 tablespoons almond extract. Divide filling equally among persimmon shells and stuff them. Refreeze. Serve partially frozen with a mint sprig garnish.

Persimmon Spice Bread

Yield: 1 loaf

1³/₄ cups all-purpose flour

1   teaspoon baking powder

¹/₂   teaspoon baking soda

¹/₄   teaspoon salt

¹/₂   cup sugar

1   teaspoon ground cinnamon

¹/₂   teaspoon ground nutmeg

¹/₂   teaspoon ground cloves

1   cup persimmon purée

¹/₃   cup skim milk

¹/₃   cup vegetable oil

¹/₂   cup egg substitute

Topping: ¹/₄ cup sugarless chunky
      peanut butter

Lightly coat 9 by 5 by 3-inch pan with vegetable cooking spray. Combine first eight ingredients in a large bowl. Make a well in the center of dry ingredients and set aside. Combine ³/₄ cup of persimmon pulp and remaining ingredients. Add moist ingredients to the dry ingredients and stir to moisten. Spoon into prepared pan. Bake at 350° for 60 minutes or until done. Cool 10 minutes in pan before removing. Remove bread and cool on wire rack.

To make topping: Mix peanut butter with remaining ¹/₄ cup persimmon purée and frost bread.

Persimmon Halloween Cookies

Yield: 1¹/₂ dozen

¹/₂   cup softened butter

1   cup sugar

1   cup persimmon pulp

2   cups all-purpose flour

1   teaspoon pumpkin pie spice

¹/₄   teaspoon salt

1   teaspoon baking powder

1   teaspoon baking soda

1¹/₂ cups M & M chocolate candies

Coat baking sheet lightly with vegetable cooking spray. Cream butter, sugar, and persimmon pulp in large bowl. Beat until fluffy. Combine next six ingredients and add to persimmon mixture. Drop dough by heaping tablespoonfuls four inches apart onto prepared cookie sheet. Lightly press dough into a 3¹/₂-inch circle with fingertips dusted with flour. Add more M & Ms to cookies if desired. Bake at 350° for 15 minutes or until brown. Cool on baking sheet 3–4 minutes. If removed from baking sheet too quickly, cookies will bend and be unattractive.

Persimmon Ice Cream Pie with Coconut Crumb Crust

Yield: 9-inch pie

Filling:

1   cup persimmon purée

1   quart softened butter pecan ice cream

1   tablespoon ground cinnamon

Garnish: Fresh persimmon slices

Follow directions for Coconut Crumb Crust on p. 65. Soften ice cream in microwave at High 10 seconds. Combine persimmon purée, softened ice cream, and cinnamon. Spoon mixture into chilled coconut crust and freeze until firm. Allow pie to stand at room temperature 5 minutes before serving. Garnish with thin persimmon slices before serving.

Persimmon Doughnut Nuggets

Yield: 1$\frac{1}{2}$ dozen

Topping: $\frac{1}{2}$ cup sugar

2   tablespoons ground cinnamon

Nuggets: 1$\frac{1}{2}$ cups all-purpose flour

1   tablespoon baking powder

$\frac{1}{2}$ teaspoon salt

$\frac{1}{3}$ cup sugar

$\frac{1}{2}$ teaspoon ground cinnamon

$\frac{1}{2}$ teaspoon ground nutmeg

$\frac{1}{4}$ teaspoon ground ginger

1   egg, beaten

$\frac{1}{2}$ cup persimmon purée

$\frac{1}{4}$ cup milk

2   tablespoons vegetable oil

1   teaspoon vanilla flavoring

Vegetable oil for frying

Combine topping ingredients in paper or plastic bag. Set aside. Combine next seven ingredients in medium bowl. Combine remaining nugget ingredients in another bowl. Add persimmon mixture to dry ingredients and stir to moisten. Pour 2 inches of oil into a heavy skillet. Heat oil to 375°. Carefully drop dough by level tablespoonfuls into hot oil. Fry until golden, turning once. Drain on paper towels and shake several nuggets at a time in the sugar/cinnamon mixture. Serve warm.

Persimmon-Rice Salad

Yield: 6 servings

3/4   cup water

1/3   cup uncooked long-grain rice

1   (7 3/4-ounce) can salmon

6   Fuyu persimmons (nonastringent, flat, light orange, crisp)

1/4   cup low-fat sour cream

1/4   cup minced watercress or fresh parsley

1   tablespoon prepared mustard

1   teaspoon paprika

1/4   cup mushroom pieces

4   cups chopped watercress or fresh spinach for salad bed

Bring water to boil in a small saucepan. Add rice, cover, reduce heat, and simmer 20 minutes or until water is absorbed and rice is tender. Drain salmon. Remove skin and bones, if desired, and flake salmon with a fork. Cut hole in stem end of persimmons and remove pulp without piercing skin. Add persimmon pulp, salmon, and remaining ingredients to the cooked rice. Stir. Stuff mixture into persimmon shells and refrigerate at least 1 hour. Serve on a bed of watercress or fresh spinach. This is a colorful luncheon salad that can be prepared in advance and refrigerated overnight.

Persimmon Snow Peas

Yield: 4 servings

1   (10-ounce) package frozen snow pea pods

2   tablespoons tangy, brown mustard

1/4   teaspoon ground pepper

1   tablespoon lime juice

2   Fuyu persimmons

Cook snow peas according to package directions. Drain and discard liquid. Combine mustard, pepper, and lime juice and mix into the snow peas. Remove stem end from the persimmons and cut fruit into 1/4-inch slices. Gently toss persimmon slices with snow peas.

Pineapple

Ananas comosus

IN PUNA, KA'U, AND KONA on the Big Island as well as at Kaupō, Maui, wild varieties of pineapple, called Wild Kailua, have been considered a native plant. The Hawaiians used the fragrant "eyes" (*maka*) of the pineapple rind for leis and also ate the fruit. About 1500, a Spanish vessel was wrecked near Kona and speculation is that it carried pineapples, native plants of tropical America, for the crew. It is possible that the Wild Kailua pineapple came from that vessel or from other Spanish vessels that found their way to the Islands. The first written account of pineapple in Hawai'i appears in Don Francisco de Paula Marin's diary in 1813, and 50 years later whalers in Kailua-Kona were provisioned with pineapple.

Smooth Cayenne is the commercial variety now grown in Hawai'i for both fresh and processed fruit. These fruits are larger and juicier than the native Wild Kailua plant. Today, pineapple ranks first in total fruit production in Hawai'i, with 25 percent of the crop sold fresh and the remaining 75 percent processed.

Another type of pineapple, different from the Smooth Cayenne, and sometimes available in Island markets, is a pineapple popularly called Sugarloaf. It is low in acid and weighs from seven to ten pounds with cream-colored, sweet flesh and a heady aroma. One distinguishing feature of this pineapple is the absence of serration on the leaves of its crown. The Sugarloaf makes a good backyard plant, producing several crops throughout the year from the original plant.

Pineapple does not grow on trees or on bushes, but got the name from its vague resemblance to the pine cone. Pineapples are a herbaceous perennial plant of the bromeliad family. "Phoenix Pear" is a translation of the Chinese name for the fruit, referring to the legendary bird that consumes itself by fire and then is renewed from its ashes. This is appropriate because the cactuslike pineapple plant grows from its own crown, the leafy portion at the top of the fruit.

Pineapple develops from a cluster of tiny, lavender flowers on a short stalk growing from the center of the leaves. It is a collective fruit, made up of many small fruits. The flowers fuse with the bracts to become fleshy and eventually form a fruit. It takes about 6 months for the pineapple to mature. The fibrous, chewy pineapple core is the original flower stalk. The tough rind, which is deep yellow or brown-green, has small, hexagonal sections that fit together like a puzzle. Each of these sections is a botanically individual fruit; they merge to form the pineapple.

Use

Selecting a ripe pineapple is not easy. When the fruit is unripe it contains no starch to convert to sugar. The starch in the plant's leaves converts into sugar and goes directly into the ripening fruit. The pineapple does not get sweeter after it is picked, but the acid within the fruit weakens. Therefore, do not keep pineapple with the expectation that it will sweeten. It is as sweet as it will get when it is picked. Hawaiian pineapples are picked at optimum sweetness and rushed to market by air to maintain peak freshness and quality. Avoid pineapples with discolored soft spots or an unpleasant odor.

Various techniques are used to find a good pineapple: pulling a leaf from the crown, thumping the fruit, judging color or the condition of the "eyes" of the pineapple. Color is a poor indicator because some varieties are naturally green. A sweet fragrance, together with a solid thud when the fruit is thumped can reveal a sweet and juicy fruit.

Like kiwi and papaya, fresh and uncooked pineapple contains an enzyme that tenderizes meat and is believed to aid digestion, but prevents coagulation when used with a protein-based gelatin. Use agar, which is a seaweed base, for molded salads.

When cutting a pineapple, notice that the "eyes" follow a spiral pattern. To use only the flesh, cut off the top and the base. Remove the rind with lengthwise cuts. Remove the "eyes" by cutting a diagonal strip around the pineapple, making a spiral groove around the fruit. If you are not fussy about the "eyes," take out the large ones with the tip of a knife or a vegetable peeler, leaving the smaller eyes intact. The pineapple can be cut lengthwise into quarters. Remove the core. The chewy core can be eaten or used for stirrers in ice tea or tropical drinks. Cut the fruit into chunks, spears, or slices.

For a pineapple shell, cut a whole, unpeeled pineapple in half, starting at the bottom, through to the crown. Cut around each half of the fruit about one-half inch from the shell. Remove the fruit and drain the shells to use as a serving bowl for salad, hot curry, dip, soup, or an appetizer.

For a pineapple boat, halve the fruit lengthwise, leaving the rind and crown intact. Cut under the core, leaving it attached at both ends. Cut under the fruit, freeing it from the rind, and cut the fruit into one-inch slices from top to bottom. Now, push the slices into an uneven edge and make certain fruit is free from the rind.

✻✻✻✻✻✻✻

Buffet Pineapple

Yield: 8 –10 servings

1　large pineapple

Optional: ½ cup triple sec or rum.

Select a large pineapple with well-developed "eyes," strong fragrance, and a solid thud when thumped. Wash and dry pineapple. Remove and reserve crown by cutting crosswise one inch from top. Remove and reserve bottom by cutting crosswise one inch from base. Use a sharp knife and remove pineapple pulp in one piece, leaving a one-half-inch shell. Cut pineapple pulp into individual serving spears and remove the central core. (The pineapple core makes excellent beverage stirrers and is considered enjoyable to chew by many Islanders.) If desired, marinate and refrigerate pineapple spears in triple sec or rum at least 1 hour. To assemble, place four sturdy, double-pointed toothpicks evenly spaced around the periphery and into the flesh of the pineapple base. Join the shell to the base, securing it snugly with the picks and fitting it correctly to obscure the cut. Drain spears and place them vertically within the shell. Top with pineapple crown.

Pineapple Dip

Yield: 2 cups

2   cups low-fat plain yogurt

1   cup 1/4-inch pineapple pieces, drained

3   tablespoons pineapple fruit spread

1/2 teaspoon ground cloves

1/2 teaspoon ground nutmeg

Optional: Substitute 1 tablespoon curry powder for cloves and nutmeg.

Combine all ingredients and chill 30 minutes before serving. Especially good as a dressing for baked potatoes, sweet potatoes, asparagus, broccoli, and as a dip for fresh fruit.

Beef and Pine Kabob Appetizer

Yield: 4 servings

1   cup low-sodium soy sauce

1/4 cup whiskey or cooking sherry

1   tablespoon shredded gingerroot or gingerroot juice

1   crushed garlic clove

1   tablespoon minced, fresh mint

3   cups chuck, sirloin, or top round tender beef cut into 1-inch cubes

1   cup fresh pineapple chunks

1   cup deseeded grapefruit chunks

3   tablespoons olive oil

1   tablespoon chopped, fresh basil leaves

3   tablespoons pineapple juice

Combine first five ingredients. Mix well and add beef chunks. Refrigerate and marinate at least 2 hours. Thread meat and fruit alternately onto skewers. Discard marinade. Blend olive oil with the fresh basil and fruit juice. Grill over medium coals 5–10 minutes, turning kabobs and basting with oil mixture. Kabobs can be served either warm or cold and are especially good for picnics.

Alternate method: Broil in oven five inches from heat for approximately 5 minutes, turning kabobs and basting with olive oil mixture until done.

Pineapple Chutney

Yield: approximately 2 quarts

$1/2$ cup granulated sugar

$1/2$ cup dark brown sugar

1 cup currants

1 cup cider vinegar

3 tiny red chilies, deseeded

2 tablespoons minced gingerroot

1 teaspoon allspice

1 tablespoon mustard seeds

$1/2$ teaspoon ground cloves

2 tablespoons tamarind concentrate

$1/2$ cup chopped onion

2 minced garlic cloves

7 cups $1/2$-inch pineapple chunks

Combine all ingredients except pineapple chunks. Bring mixture to a boil. Add pineapple chunks and return to a boil. Reduce heat and simmer, uncovered, stirring often to prevent sticking until slightly thickened, about 45 minutes. Place pineapple chutney into sterilized jars or freezer bags. Cover immediately, cool, and refrigerate up to 1 month or freeze up to 6 months.

Microwave method: After adding pineapple chunks and returning the mixture to a boil, remove 4 cups of the chutney to a 2-quart pourable glass measure. Microwave at High to desired consistency, about 10 minutes. Repeat procedure.

Stuffed Pineapple with Chutney Salad

Yield: 6–8 servings

1 large pineapple

2 cups cooked chicken, turkey, ham, imitation crab, or tiny shrimp

$1/2$ cup chopped celery

1 cup pineapple or mango chutney

1 cup low-cholesterol mayonnaise or to taste

1 tablespoon lime zest

Remove crown from pineapple and save. Remove bottom of pineapple, peel pineapple, and remove eyes. Start at top of fruit and remove the core. Hollow out the pineapple, leaving a one-inch shell of the fruit. Remove pineapple fruit and dice. Mix chicken, celery, chutney, mayonnaise, and zest in large bowl. Add pineapple chunks and mix thoroughly. Pack the pineapple shell with salad, wrap, and chill at least 2 hours. To serve, cut pineapple horizontally into one-half-inch rings and reassemble with top for buffet service. Or serve slices on individual salad plates, using coarsely chopped watercress or red lettuce as a bed for the salad.

Pineapple Mustard

2   cups Dijon-style mustard

5   tablespoons pineapple chutney

Optional: 1 tablespoon sherry.

Mix thoroughly. Flavors intensify if refrigerated at least 2 hours before using. Refrigerate up to 1 month. Serve on sandwiches, hot dogs, and hamburgers. This tropical fruit mustard makes a unique hostess gift when placed in an attractive container.

Pineapple Marinade

Yield: 4 cups

Marinade made with pineapple not only adds flavor to beef, poultry, and fish, but it tenderizes as well. Both pineapple and papaya have enzymes that break down animal protein and are especially good to include in a marinade. Use a glass container or a plastic bag for marinating and always refrigerate the food while it is marinating. Food should be marinated at least 1 hour before cooking to blend the flavors. Do not marinate food again at the very end of the cooking process. Make certain to allow enough time for the marinade to cook. Serve remaining marinade only after it has been boiled. Do not save marinade to use again.

1   crushed garlic clove

1   tablespoon minced gingerroot

1   carambola or ¼ cup lime juice

2   cups pineapple or papaya chunks

1   teaspoon cardamon or 1 teaspoon Chinese five spice

½   teaspoon rosemary

½   teaspoon tarragon

1   teaspoon coarse black pepper

1   tablespoon brown sugar

2   cups low-sodium soy sauce

Optional: ¼ cup whiskey.

Chop garlic clove and gingerroot in food processor using knife blade. Add fruit, spices, and brown sugar. Purée. Stir in soy sauce. Refrigerate, marinating food at least 1 hour before cooking.

Pineapple Fruit Spread

This fruit spread has a fresh flavor, color, and texture that is cooked away in traditional pineapple jam. Some fruit is suitable for jam making with unflavored gelatin as a thickening agent, but pineapple is not. Enzymes in pineapple, papaya, and kiwi break down the animal protein contained in gelatin. Use agar instead. It can be purchased in most supermarkets, health-food stores, or Asian markets.

1   cup pineapple juice

1   stick agar or 4 tablespoons agar flakes

3   cups fresh ½-inch pineapple chunks

¼   cup orange zest

½   teaspoon ground ginger

1   teaspoon ground cloves

Optional: 2 tablespoons honey.

Warm pineapple juice in 2-quart glass measure in the microwave at High 1 minute or on the stove top over low heat. Break agar into pieces and dissolve it in the warm pineapple juice. Let stand 3 minutes. Stir. Completely dissolve agar in the microwave on High for 30-second intervals or on the stove top over medium heat.

Mix pineapple, orange zest, ginger, and cloves in a large bowl. Add the agar mixture and stir. Taste; add honey if desired.

To make a hot pineapple fruit spread, mix these ingredients into the fruit:

3   small, red chilies, minced or 2 tablespoons chopped green chilies

1   teaspoon coriander seeds

½   teaspoon cumin seeds

½   teaspoon cardamom seeds

Pineapple Salsa

Yield: 4 cups

2 cups diced pineapple

¼ cup lime juice or lemon juice

1 cup shredded red or yellow onion

1 (2¼ ounce) can sliced ripe olives, drained

1 teaspoon ground cumin

1 teaspoon coriander seeds

1 teaspoon black pepper

1 (4½) ounce can diced green chilies or fresh chilies to taste

2 tablespoons minced Chinese parsley (cilantro) or parsley

Optional: 1 crushed garlic clove or to taste.

Combine all ingredients. Flavors blend when refrigerated 2 hours or overnight. Pineapple makes a superb salsa to serve with fish, poultry, meat, and tortilla dishes. The flavor improves with age, so make it ahead and store in the refrigerator up to a week.

Teriyaki-Pineapple Meatloaf

Yield: 6 servings

Meat loaf:

2 pounds ground turkey or chicken

½ cup diced onion

½ cup diced sweet pepper

½ cup sliced celery

1 cup quick oats, uncooked or 1 cup whole-wheat bread crumbs

2 egg whites or ½ cup drained tofu

1 tablespoon prepared mustard

1 tablespoon Worcestershire sauce

¼ cup low-sodium soy sauce

¾ cup pineapple chutney

Combine all meat loaf ingredients in large bowl, except topping ingredients. Mix thoroughly. In small bowl, blend together the topping ingredients. Lightly coat broiler pan and rack or 2-quart microwave tube pan with vegetable cooking spray. Shape meat mixture into a loaf and place on prepared broiler rack to allow fat to drain. Spread on topping sauce. Bake at 350° for 1 hour or until done. Remove from pan and let stand 5–10 minutes before serving.

Microwave method: Follow recipe instructions for combining ingredients

Topping:

¼ cup low-sodium soy sauce

½ cup catsup

2 tablespoons pineapple chutney

and making topping. Shape meat mixture in prepared microwave tube pan. Microwave at High 15 minutes. Pour off liquid. Spread on topping sauce and microwave at High 5 minutes. Check for doneness. Let stand covered 5 minutes.

Pineapple Ecstacy

Yield: 6 servings

This showy dessert is good for a buffet or table service.

1 large pineapple, crown intact

1 quart banana or other fruit ice cream

½ cup drained mango chunks

½ cup drained lychee halves

1 cup macadamia nut bits

Optional: ¼ cup rum; 1 passion fruit. Cut top from passion fruit and scoop out pulp. Serve passion fruit pulp with seeds in a small bowl as sauce for the dessert.

If desired, flavor ice cream with rum and refreeze. Cut off pineapple crown including the top two inches of fruit. Scoop out pineapple pulp without damaging or cutting through the rind. Dice pulp and mix 1 cup drained chunks with mango and lychee. Refrigerate remaining pineapple chunks for another use. To assemble pineapple, layer the inside of the pineapple shell with two inches of ice cream, a layer of fruit, and a layer of ¼ cup nuts; repeat the procedure to the top. Replace crown. Serve on a bed of ice to keep ice cream chilled.

Pineapple Tea

Yield: approximately 50 cups

2½ tablespoons whole cloves

5   cinnamon sticks

¼   pound orange pekoe tea

½   cup dried or crystallized pine-apple

¼   cup crystallized ginger

1   teaspoon nutmeg

Use a food processor with a metal blade or a mortar and pestle. Crush the cloves and cinnamon sticks until well blended. Add remaining ingredients and process until finely blended. Store in tightly covered container.

To brew fruit tea, place 1 teaspoon of pineapple tea for each serving into an infuser. Add ¾ cup boiling water for each serving to the teapot. Steep 2–4 minutes or until tea reaches desired strength.

Pineapple Tea Gift Basket

Through the centuries, pineapple has been a sought-after exotic fruit. In Europe, it was the stylish fruit of the 1700s and was grown for Louis XIV at Versailles in hothouses. In colonial America, the pineapple became a symbol for hospitality.

Line a basket with a kapa (tapa) cloth napkin. Include a pineapple tea blend in an attractive tin, a small jar of pineapple fruit spread, a tea infuser, or an individual teapot.

Giant Pineapple-Nut Muffins

Yield: 6 large muffins

2   cups bran flakes

1   cup milk

1   cup all-purpose flour

2   teaspoons baking powder

½   teaspoon baking soda

½   cup firmly packed brown sugar

⅔   cup pineapple tidbits, drained

⅓   cup coarsely chopped macadamia nuts

¼   cup melted margarine

1   egg, beaten

Lightly coat with vegetable cooking spray muffin pan or 6 custard cups. Combine bran flakes and milk in a medium bowl and let stand 5 minutes. Combine flour, baking powder, and baking soda in a separate bowl. Stir together 5 tablespoons brown sugar, fruit, nuts, margarine, and egg and add to the bran mixture. Blend flour mixture into the bran and fruit. Spoon batter into prepared muffin pans. Press remaining 3 tablespoons of brown sugar onto tops of the muffins. Bake at 400° for 20–25 minutes or until done. Remove from pans and cool on wire rack.

Piña Colada Monkey Bread

Yield: 10–12 servings

This streamlined version of monkey bread eliminates the preparation of a yeast bread and substitutes refrigerated biscuits to make a fun brunch or luncheon treat.

1/2	cup brown sugar
1/4	cup granulated sugar
4	(10-ounce) cans refrigerated buttermilk biscuits
3	cups 1/4-inch pineapple pieces, drained
1	tablespoon orange zest
6	tablespoons margarine
1/4	cup shredded coconut
1	teaspoon almond flavoring
1	teaspoon coconut flavoring

Preheat oven to 350°. Lightly coat 10-inch tube pan with vegetable cooking spray. Mix sugars in medium bowl. Dip biscuits into sugars, coating them sparingly. Cut biscuits into quarters and place one-fourth of the biscuit pieces and one-fourth of the pineapple pieces in a layer in the prepared tube pan. Repeat the procedure three more times. In a saucepan, combine the remaining sugars and the additional ingredients. Cook over low heat to dissolve sugars and to melt margarine. Pour mixture over biscuits and pineapple in the tube pan. Bake for 30 minutes at 350° or until done. Cover top with foil the last 10 minutes of baking. Cool in pan 5 minutes before removing monkey bread to a serving platter. Serve warm. May be reheated.

Spirited Tropical Fruit

This recipe provides fruit and sauce that are delicious over cake, ice cream, sherbet, and puddings. It is also good in meringue or chocolate cups. Fruit is added to a jar in layers and covered with rum. Upon completion, the fruit is a quick dessert and the rum can be decanted for an exceptional gift.

Chunks of fresh fruit (pineapple, firm papaya, lychee, kumquat, firm mango, carambola, guava, or firm persimmon)

Dark or light rum

Optional: Honey.

To make the first layer, cut fresh pineapple or any other fruits into 1-inch chunks. Sweeten with honey, if desired. Put a three-inch layer of fruit into a large glass jar with a tight lid. Add rum to cover fruit by 1/2 inch. Refrigerate. Wait 1–2 days for the fruit to mellow before adding another three-inch layer of fruit. As fruit is added, replenish rum to cover fruit by 1/2 inch. Continue to sweeten if desired. Keep refrigerated. Fruit is at maximum flavor in about 6 weeks.

Pomegranate

Punica granatum

THE POMEGRANATE, a highly portable fruit with a leathery skin, does not bruise easily and has juicy, red kernels that are an excellent thirst quencher. It is an ancient fruit, a symbol of fertility, good fortune, and immortality in many cultures. It is mentioned in the Old Testament as growing in the Hanging Gardens of Babylon. Pomegranate also appears in Greek mythology, where it explains the changing seasons. It was pomegranate seeds that Persephone ate that gave Pluto power over her and prevented her return to earth, thus causing winter.

The fruit's origin is the Middle East, where Mohammad prescribed the pomegranate as a cleanser for hate and evil. It is widely cultivated in the Mediterranean area and is Spain's national emblem. Granada in Spain takes its name from the fruit and has an avenue of pomegranate trees that were planted by the Moors.

Pomegranate is a spiny shrub about six feet tall and can be grown as a hedge or as an ornamental. Its young leaves are reddish, and its small, showy flowers are orange-red. The attractive fruit is round, reddish gold, and two to five inches in diameter. The fruit has a crown effect on its blossom end. The juicy kernels inside the pomegranate are held in a cream-colored, bitter membrane that is not edible. Be careful of the fruit's juice because it is indelible and can be used as a fabric dye. There is a dwarf pomegranate grown as a container plant mainly for foliage and flowers that also has small, edible fruits.

Use

Choose richly colored fruit which is heavy and smooth. The larger the fruit, the greater proportion of juicy pulp. Pomegranate can be kept in the refrigerator for 2–3 months. The seeds (kernels) can be frozen and last 2–3 months.

One method for removing pomegranate seeds is to cut out the blossom end, removing some of the white pith. Do not break the red pulp around the seeds. Score the skin into quarters. Break fruit into halves and then halve again following the score lines. Then, bend back the rind and pull out the seeds. The fun in eating a pomegranate is crunching the seeds. Fastidious eaters who avoid fruit seeds will not enjoy pomegranate. A juice extractor or a food processor can be used to extract juice from the pulp. If desired, the juice can be strained.

Pomegranate makes beautiful sorbet, icing, marinade, salad dressing, soup, and sauce for fish and chicken. Use the seeds to garnish fruit salad, dessert, appetizers, and to color and flavor icings, puddings, and sauces. Pomegranate seeds add color, texture, and tartness to any dish. Canned or bottled pomegranate juice is not uncommon. Depending on size, two or three pomegranates make 1 cup of juice.

❊❊❊❊❊❊❊

Pomegranate Syrup (Grenadine) Yield: 2 cups

Recognized as a basic bar ingredient, this natural product makes a wonderful gift, replacing the synthetic, commercial syrup that usually contains no pomegranate. This syrup is good in beverages, salad dressings, entrées, and dessert sauces.

4	pomegranates
¼	cup honey

Remove seeds from pomegranates, place them in container of food processor, and process using knife blade. Simmer honey and pomegranate pulp over low heat 3 minutes. Stir well. Strain to remove seeds. Pour into sterilized jar, cool, cover, and refrigerate.

Tropical Ice Cream Cookies

Scoop one flavor or a variety of tropical fruit ice cream—lychee, mango, pineapple, guava—into 2½-inch balls. Lightly roll the ice cream balls in crushed chocolate cookie crumbs. Cover and freeze until firm. Arrange in individual serving dishes or a large serving bowl. Top with warm pomegranate syrup. The warm, garnet-colored pomegranate topping makes a spectacular dessert.

Pomegranate Soup

Yield: 8 cups

1 onion, diced

½ cup lentils

6 cups water

1 cup brown rice

½ cup chopped parsley or Chinese parsley (cilantro)

2 cups chopped fresh spinach

2 cups pomegranate juice (3–4 pomegranates)

2 teaspoons oregano

2 teaspoons basil

Dash of bottled chili pepper sauce to taste

Optional: 1 cup spicy sausage or 1 cup ham cut into 1-inch pieces.

Lightly coat dutch oven or large cooking pan with vegetable cooking spray. Sauté onion in prepared pan and add lentils and water. Bring to a boil and simmer over low heat 30 minutes. Add all remaining ingredients. Simmer for 1 hour. Ladle into individual soup bowls and garnish. Best served hot.

Pomegranate Salad Dressing

Yield: 2 cups

1 cup macadamia nut oil or olive oil

1 tablespoon honey

½ cup red wine vinegar

1 teaspoon prepared spicy mustard

1 tablespoon sesame seeds

1 teaspoon ground ginger

1 cup pomegranate seeds

Place all ingredients except fruit seeds into blender or food processor container. Use metal blade to mix. Add pomegranate seeds and process only to the appearance of very coarse pepper. Chill at least 1 hour before serving. This dressing is good on fruit salads, green leaf salads, and vegetables.

Variation: To make a creamy salad dressing, stir ½ cup low-cholesterol mayonnaise or ½ cup low-fat yogurt into finished dressing.

Pomegranate Sauce

Yield: 1 cup

2 pomegranates
1/4 cup macadamia nut bits
1/4 cup orange juice
2 teaspoons arrowroot
1 tablespoon honey
1 teaspoon marjoram
1 tablespoon minced parsley
1 tablespoon coarse black pepper

Remove seeds from pomegranates. Use knife blade in food processor to crush pomegranate seeds and extract juice. Stir remaining ingredients into the pomegranate juice in the food processor bowl. Place bowl in microwave and warm at High 3 minutes. Stir well. Use on lamb, ham, beef, and chicken.

Alternate method: Place pomegranate pulp and all remaining ingredients into a small saucepan. Stir and warm sauce over low heat. Do not boil.

Pomegranate Vinegar

Yield: 4 cups

1 cup pomegranate or passion fruit seeds and pulp
4 cups vinegar
1/4 cup honey

Crush seeds and pulp with knife blade in a food processor. Use a nonaluminum pan to bring vinegar and honey almost to a boil over medium heat. Stir pulp and seeds into the container and cover tightly. Let stand covered at room temperature 48 hours. Strain vinegar to remove seed particles. Refrigerate vinegar up to 6 months. This fruit vinegar is a beautiful color and can be used in salad dressings, sauces, and marinades.

Pomegranate Relish

Yield: 3 cups

3 pomegranates
1/2 cup cooked wild rice or cooked bulgur
1 sweet red or green pepper, diced
1/3 cup diced celery
1/2 cup diced onion
1/4 cup cider vinegar
2 tablespoons brown sugar
1 tablespoon mustard seed
2 teaspoons allspice
1 tablespoon minced gingerroot
2 tablespoons minced fresh mint

Remove seeds from pomegranates. Crush pomegranate seeds and pulp with the knife blade in the food processor. Put pomegranate pulp and remaining ingredients in a large bowl. Stir to blend flavors. Chill at least 1 hour before serving. This is a colorful relish for the holidays. Serve it with turkey, ham, and beef.

Pomegranate Fruitsicles

Yield: 6 fruitsicles

2   pomegranates
1   cup mashed banana
¼   cup guava juice or pineapple juice

Remove seeds from pomegranates. Crush pomegranate seeds and pulp with the knife blade in a food processor. Add banana and fruit juice and blend to desired consistency. Fill molds and freeze. A commercial plastic set of containers may be used for home production. It includes tray, cups, covers, and plastic sticks for making six fruitsicles.

Pomegranate Marinade

Yield: 2 cups

1   cup crushed pomegranate pulp
     and seeds
2   tablespoons Worcestershire sauce
1   tablespoon rosemary
¼   cup pineapple juice
2   crushed garlic cloves

Combine all ingredients and marinate food at least 1 hour before cooking. This easy-to-prepare marinade gives chicken and seafood a wonderful color.

Red Sunset Sherbet

Yield: 6 servings

2¼ cups nonfat buttermilk
1   cup ripe mango chunks
½   cup pomegranate pulp and seeds
1   (6-ounce) can thawed frozen
     passion fruit concentrate, undiluted
1 banana, peeled and sliced
Garnish: 2 tablespoons crème de
     menthe per serving

Combine all ingredients in container of food processor or electric blender. Process with knife blade until smooth. Freeze mixture in an ice cream freezer according to manufacturer's instructions. Serve in chilled stemmed glasses. This is a rainbow of tropical flavors.

Alternate method: Pour mixture into an eight-inch-square pan and freeze until firm. Stir several times during the freezing process.

New Market Fruits

NOT LONG AGO, avocado, kiwi, and papaya were unfamiliar and scarce in many markets. Today, these fruits and appropriate recipes are commonplace. The new market fruits in this chapter are not newly discovered fruits. Indeed, many are considered ordinary and are grown by backyard gardeners in Hawai'i, Florida, and California. Many, however, seem new and unusual because they have not yet received wide retail distribution.

Advertising by the growers' associations promotes consumer awareness. In addition, immigrants bringing food tastes from their homeland and travelers having experienced new taste adventures provide a ready market for diverse foods. This expands the diet and choices of local residents. Food magazines respond to requests for "how to" information on "new to the market" fruits by publishing exciting recipes and articles about exotic fruits, which, in turn, create more demand in restaurants and markets.

Ethnic food stores in Hawai'i and throughout the American mainland usually have a selection of tropical fruits. More supermarkets are selling exotic fruits. Nurseries in appropriate climates sell tropical and subtropical fruit trees, and university extension services supply brochures and have agents on staff to assist the home gardener.

Atemoya	*Annona atemoya*
Cherimoya	*Annona cherimola*
Soursop	*Annona muricata*
Sweetsop	*Annona squamosa*

These four fruits belong to the custard-apple (Annonaceae) family. There are similarities between the familiar magnolia family and the annonas. Both are considered primitive, in the evolutionary sense, with the magnolias at the base of the family tree. Annonas are one of the earliest recorded New World fruits. There are about sixty species of them and, when ripe, all have a thick, soft, inedible skin with shiny, watermelonlike seeds that should not be eaten because they contain a toxic substance.

The pulp of the annonas is silky smooth and cream colored and gives the fruit its common name, custard apple. The fruit should not be overripe; it should be used when it is as soft as a ripe avocado. The green skin bruises easily and is bumpy with protuberances or indentations. The atemoya, cherimoya, and sweetsop are about four inches in diameter and weigh two pounds.

Annonas are grown commercially and in home gardens in Hawai'i, Florida, California, Australia, New Zealand, South America, and Spain. Their season in Hawai'i is customarily February through September, and all varieties of annonas may appear in the stores labeled "moya." They are best eaten chilled and combined in fruit salads, smoothies, beverages, and ices, or used as a dessert sauce or salad dressing.

Purchase unripe, hard fruit and ripen at room temperature for 2–4 days before refrigerating. The skin may darken when refrigerated, but the pulp is unaffected. To extract the pulp from the seeds, strain it through a sieve or use a food mill and discard the seeds. Once the pulp is free of seeds, it can be puréed or cut into chunks and may be frozen for 6 to 9 months.

The atemoya can be heart-shaped or round and is a natural hybrid, a cross between the cherimoya and the sweetsop (sugar apple). The atemoya's bumpy skin is light green, and its juicy flesh is a combination of pleasantly tart and sweet.

Cherimoya means "cold seeds" in the ancient Quechua (Incan) language. It is related to the papaw, the native American tree growing wild in the midwestern states of Indiana, Nebraska, and Michigan. The cherimoya is heart-shaped with a dull, light green skin, and a convex, bumpy surface typical of all the moyas. Its sharp, slightly vanilla flavor is unique and has been described as a blend of pineapple and banana. This fruit is rated superior by many connoisseurs.

The soursop is twice as big as the atemoya and cherimoya; it can be eight inches long and weigh five or more pounds. It is heart-shaped with a leathery, dark green skin covered with soft, hooked, fleshy spines. The pulp is aromatic with a tart, custard-banana flavor.

The sweetsop, also known as the sugar apple, is the most widely distributed member of the annonas. It has pale yellow, very sweet flesh.

The fruit has large, prominent knobs that separate when it is ripe. The segmented skin is bluish green, and it resembles an artichoke.

Durian   *Durio zibethinus*

Jokingly called the "schizoid fruit," durian combines an obnoxious smell with a delectable and sweet-tasting flesh that devotees proclaim as heavenly. The smell of an open durian has been called "unendurable." This highly prized fruit is grown in Southeast Asia, especially Thailand, Malaysia, the Philippines, and Indonesia. Supposedly, elephants and tigers are fond of durian and can detect it from afar by its unique odor.

It is not easy to export fresh durian, and unusual precautions are taken to prevent a rupture in the fruit. Now and then, fresh durian is available in Honolulu, and canned fruit is not difficult to find. This green-colored fruit, eight to twelve inches long, football-shaped with short, woody spikes, can weigh ten pounds and be costly. Fresh fruit will last a week if refrigerated. Durian is also sold in the form of a flavored candy and as a dehydrated powder for making durian ice cream. The pulp can be puréed and used for cakes, cookies, and other desserts.

Jackfruit   *Artocarpus heterophyllus*

This fruit, also spelled jakfruit, is native to rain forests from India to the Malay Peninsula and is a close relative to breadfruit. Like the breadfruit and pineapple, it is a collective fruit of fused individual fruitlets. The name "jack" was given to the fruit by the Portuguese in the sixteenth century because it sounded like *tsjaka*, the Malay word for the fruit.

Jackfruit is prized for its sweet and delicious flavor, and its juicy, cream-colored, golden, or pink flesh. Among some cultures, it is rumored to have aphrodisiac qualities. One variety of jackfruit has firm, crisp pulp and another has soft, melting pulp. If buying fresh fruit, select one that has a sweet aroma because an unpleasant odor indicates overripe fruit.

Jackfruit, the world's largest fruit, is oblong and firm with a light, green, bumpy skin that changes to yellow-brown when ripe. It can be three feet long by eighteen inches wide and weigh forty to fifty pounds, although exceptional fruit can weigh 100 pounds. The tree can bear 150–250 fruits a year suspended on strong stalks along its main trunk and larger branches. Each fruit can have as many as 100 one-inch, kidney-shaped seeds, which, when boiled or roasted, are more highly valued than the pulp. The fleshy segment that encloses the seed is the choicest part of the fruit. When it is available, jackfruit can be purchased whole, as chunks, or just the seed segments. Immature jackfruit is prepared fried, roasted, or boiled like a vegetable. Ripe jackfruit, prepared like a fruit, is good mixed into curries and used for fruit salads, preserves, and syrup.

Mammee Apple   *Mammea americana*

This tree, also spelled Mamey Apple, was introduced into Hawai'i in 1816 by Alexander Adams, the captain of King Kamehameha I's merchant ship, *Ka'ahumanu*. The beautiful orange-colored flesh of the mammee makes it a favorite for photographs in food magazines. It is native to tropical America and the West Indies.

The fruit is round, about four to eight inches in diameter, with rough, golden brown, thick skin. The sweet, orange flesh is apricot-flavored and surrounds one to four large, brown seeds. It is delicious raw, made into jams and jellies, or puréed for smoothies and dessert sauces.

Mangosteen   *Garcinia mangostana*

Called the "queen of tropical fruits," and Malaysia's most delicious fruit, mangosteen has been cultivated in Southeast Asia for several centuries. The tree bears its first crop after 10 years. The smooth, deep purple fruit, about three inches in diameter, has five pearly white segments that are the texture and consistency of lychee. It does not resemble a mango in taste or appearance.

This fruit is best used fresh as a dessert delicacy. Buy firm fruit and serve it whole, allowing guests to enjoy the pink insides before the color fades. To serve, cut around the circumference of the fruit, dividing it in half. The sections are easily removed. Served with a glass of wine or champagne, mangosteen makes a superlative dessert.

Longan   *Euphoria longana*

The longan (also called Dragon's Eye), rambutan, and lychee all belong to the same family, Sapindaceae. The longan is known as the "little brother" of the lychee and is native to southern China and India. In Hawai'i, it grows faster and more vigorously than the lychee. The fruit is round or oval and is a little larger than an olive. The thin, rough, caramel-colored shell is easily peeled. The juicy, white translucent pulp clings to a large, round and smooth, deep brown seed. The longan's flesh is sweeter but not as juicy as the lychee's.

The longan is best eaten raw, but canned longan is good in fruit salads and fruit cocktails. Fruits freeze well or can be refrigerated for several weeks.

Rambutan   *Nephelium lappaceum*

The rambutan, described as an "unkempt hedgehog," is native to the Malay Peninsula. *Rambut*, "hair" in Malay, describes the soft, bristling spines that give the fruit its nickname, "hairy lychee." The rambutan's reddish skin can have green, red, pink, or yellow hairs (soft spines) growing from it. The leathery skin is not prickly and peels easily.

Rambutan, slightly larger than a lychee, is called the "lychee of the tropics." Its sweet flesh is translucent and its texture resembles that of a lychee although the flavor is slightly different. Select rambutan that are not brown, dry, or soft. Choose the brightest fruit with the fleshiest spines because the skin darkens with age. Rambutan is also sold peeled and canned. It can be used in fruit salads, dessert sauces, and in sauces with chicken, duck, or seafood.

Sapodilla   *Manilkara zapota*

Anything that is described as "melting with the sweet perfumes of honey, jasmine and lily of the valley" has to be good. Even the sapodilla's black seeds with a thin white stripe are unusual. The flesh, a honey color with the hint of brown sugar, has the creamy texture of a banana. Sapodilla, also known as ciku or naseberry, is also described as a "peach in cream" and a "pear dipped in brown sugar."

The russet, round fruit, about the size of a peach, has a thin, edible skin; it should feel like a ripe kiwi, firm yet yielding to the touch. Unripe fruit contains tannin and is bitter. Sapodilla is the fruit of the Central American chicle tree, which produces latex, so it should be washed carefully before using to remove all traces of sticky latex. The fruit is good raw, or used for cake fillings, dessert sauces, sherbets, and custards.

Sapote

There are several fruits popularly called "sapote." Although they are all native to tropical America, they can be dissimilar and may even be from different families. Therefore, it is necessary to identify a sapote with a color or other word modifier.

The black sapote (*Diospyros digyna*), the "chocolate pudding fruit," has rich, sweet, chocolate brown flesh, and a greenish brown

skin. Although it is called sapote, it is in the same family and has similar characteristics as the Oriental persimmon (*D. kaki*). It is also called black persimmon. Black sapote blends beautifully with a small amount of liqueur, rum, or vanilla flavoring to intensify the fruit's delicate flavor. It may require 7–14 days to ripen and should be kept in a cool, dry place. Suddenly, after remaining hard for days, the fruit becomes marshmallow soft. Cut it into wedges from blossom to stem, scoop out the pulp, and remove the seeds. Black sapote makes a wonderful mousse and is good in cake, bread, and ice cream. It freezes well. This fruit contains about four times more vitamin C than an orange.

The white sapote (*Casimiroa edulis*) has bright green skin that changes to light yellow as it ripens. The creamy, soft pale yellow or white flesh has a sweet, melting flavor resembling custard. The fruit, also called casimiroa, is about the size of a tomato and has a thin, papery skin and two to five sizeable seeds. It is in the citrus family. Hard fruit ripens in about a week and can be refrigerated, and the pulp can be securely sealed and frozen up to 6 months. Casimiroa is excellent eaten alone or as a dessert fruit with cake or ice cream, or made into milk shakes, ices, and fruit salads.

Star Apple   *Chrysophyllum cainito*

This is another tropical American tree belonging to the same family (Sapotaceae) as the sapodilla, mamey (red) sapote, green sapote, and egg fruit. It is also known as caimito and the Mexican custard apple. It is a popular fruit in the West Indies and is cultivated in Thailand and the Philippines.

The tree is striking and graceful, with glossy green leaves that are velvety copper on the underside. The fruit resembles an apple without the indentation at the blossom end, and it has an inedible, thick, purple or light green skin. Yields from young trees can be heavy, up to 100 fruits in a season.

Slicing the caimito horizontally reveals a star-shaped pattern formed by five or more edible black, glossy seeds. The flesh is sweet, white, and rather translucent. Star apple is good blended with fruit juices, puréed as a fruit sauce for salads and desserts, or sprinkled with a few drops of lime juice and eaten straight from the skin.

Island-Style Marinade

Yield: 3 cups

1   minced garlic clove
1   tablespoon minced gingerroot
1   cup moya, guava, or passion fruit purée
1   tablespoon lime zest
5   tablespoons hoisin sauce
1   tablespoon sesame oil
2   cups low-sodium soy sauce
1   tablespoon honey
1   teaspoon Chinese chili sauce or ¼ teaspoon dried chilies

Optional: ¼ cup whiskey.

Chop garlic clove and gingerroot in food processor using knife blade. Stir in fruit purée. Add remaining ingredients and mix thoroughly. Refrigerate, marinating food at least 1 hour before cooking. Because this marinade has an oil base, it is particularly good for grilled foods.

Moya Sherbet

Yield: 4 servings

1   (8-ounce) carton plain low-fat yogurt
¼   cup orange juice
2   tablespoons honey
2   cups moya purée
1   teaspoon almond extract

Mix all ingredients to a creamy consistency. Pour into an 8-inch-square pan and freeze until almost firm. Break mixture into large pieces and process in blender or food processor until fluffy but not thawed. Return mixture to pan or put into serving dishes and freeze until firm.

Moya Creamy Salad Dressing

Yield: 2 cups

½ cup low-fat sour cream

½ cup low-fat cottage cheese

⅔ cup moya purée

1 tablespoon honey

⅛ teaspoon ground white pepper

Combine all ingredients in container of an electric blender or food processor and process until smooth. Cover and chill thoroughly. The rich, tart flavor of this salad dressing blends perfectly with a fresh fruit salad or avocado halves.

Fruit Flambé

Yield: 6 servings

This dramatic dessert is amazingly easy to prepare. It is good with one special fruit ('ōhelo or mammee apple) or with a mixture of tropical fruits.

2 tablespoons butter

1 tablespoon brown sugar

Juice from half a lime

2 cups firm fruit chunks, well drained

½ cup brandy or half liqueur and half brandy

Fruit preparation: Some fruits need a longer cooking time than others. If using 'ōhelo, treat them like cranberries. Bananas should not be overcooked. Carambola, lychee, mango, mammee apple, papaya, pineapple, tangerine segments, and pummelo segments can all be cooked approximately the same length of time.

Place butter, brown sugar, and lime juice in a skillet or chafing dish over moderate heat. Cook 1 minute to dissolve sugar. Add fruit, stir gently, and cook for 2 minutes. Warm brandy in microwave at High for 20 seconds in a microwave-safe container with a handle. Or warm brandy in a small, long-handled pan over low heat. Do not overheat because the alcohol evaporates and the brandy will not flame. Ignite brandy with a long match, making certain not to hover over the pan. Pour flaming liquid over the fruit mixture. Stir gently until flames die down. Serve immediately over ice cream, sherbet, or frozen yogurt.

Exotic Fruit Soufflé

Yield: 6 servings

This showy dessert is perfect for exotic fruits. Expect dessert soufflés to be softer than entrée soufflés. As a soufflé cools, it deflates. Serve immediately.

¼ cup sugar

2 tablespoons cornstarch

1 tablespoon instant coffee granules

¾ cup sapodilla, black sapote, or mammee apple purée

¼ cup evaporated skim milk

1 tablespoon coffee-flavored liqueur

1 teaspoon vanilla flavoring

6 egg whites, at room temperature

½ teaspoon cream of tartar

¼ teaspoon ground cinnamon

Coat bottom only of 2½-quart soufflé dish with cooking spray and sprinkle with 1 teaspoon sugar. Combine sugar, cornstarch, and coffee granules in medium saucepan. Stir in fruit purée and milk. Cook and stir over medium heat until very thick. Remove from heat and stir in liqueur and vanilla. Transfer mixture to a large mixing bowl. Cover with plastic wrap directly on mixture to keep warm. Beat egg whites, cream of tartar, and cinnamon in large mixing bowl at high speed of electric mixer until stiff peaks form. Fold one-third of egg white mixture into fruit mixture. Carefully fold in remaining egg white mixture. Spoon into prepared dish. Bake at 375° 20–25 minutes or until puffed and golden.

Moya Bulgur Muffins

Yield: 1½ dozen

½ cup boiling water

¼ cup cracked wheat (bulgur)

1 cup moya purée

⅓ cup margarine

⅔ cup sugar

1 egg, beaten

2 cups flour

1 teaspoon baking soda

2 teaspoons ground cinnamon

1 teaspoon ground allspice

½ teaspoon salt

⅓ cup sesame seeds

Pour boiling water over cracked wheat and let stand 20 minutes. Stir in moya purée. Cream margarine and gradually add sugar, beating at medium speed of an electric mixer until fluffy. Add egg and beat well. Combine remaining ingredients in a small bowl. Add flour mixture to the creamed mixture alternately with moya purée mixture. Lightly coat muffin pans with vegetable cooking spray. Spoon batter into prepared pans, filling three-fourths full. Bake at 375° for 15 minutes or until golden brown. Remove from pans immediately.

Kama'āina Favorites

THE FRUITS DESCRIBED in this chapter have long been available in Hawai'i and are particularly liked by kama'āinas (persons born in the Islands) and long-time residents. The 'ōhelo is endemic to the Islands, others were brought by the early Polynesian settlers, and some were introduced after the discovery of the Islands by Europeans. A few fruits may be uncommon, but most can be found readily if one knows where and when to look.

The Polynesians who immigrated to Hawai'i became known as Hawaiians, and brought with them knowledge about plants that was useful for food, medicinal, and religious purposes. Of the twenty-seven plant species introduced during the immigration, many were edible, including the following fruits: banana, breadfruit, coconut, kukui, and mountain apple.

Coffee   *Coffea arabica*

The first coffee plants in Hawai'i were in Don Francisco de Paula Marin's gardens in 1813. Coffee, native to tropical Africa, was widely cultivated and naturalized on all Hawaiian Islands by the mid-1800s. In 1828, the first coffee plantation was started in Kona on the Big Island, where the industry continues to thrive.

Kona coffee has a worldwide reputation as a mellow, smooth coffee lacking the acidity found in coffees grown at higher altitudes. It is known for its delicate, subtle bouquet. The altitude where Kona coffee grows is about 2,000 feet; elsewhere in the world coffee grows up to 6,000 feet. Kaua'i has harvested its first commercial crop in over 100 years, and coffee production on Kaua'i is expected to increase steadily as its young orchards mature.

The coffee plant is a shrub or small tree growing to about fifteen feet. Its leaves are oval, thin, and glossy green. The fragrant, white flowers grow in thick clusters and make a showy display, particularly in a field of coffee trees. In the Kona district, trees flower in March and April and fruit in the fall. They bear after 3 years and are usually profitable for 30 years. In Hawai'i, coffee trees are pruned to facilitate berry picking. Most coffee plantations in the Islands are family farm operations.

Kona coffee is sold both as 100 percent pure Kona coffee or as a blend with other coffees. It takes approximately 500 pounds of coffee fruits to produce 100 pounds of roasted coffee beans. The fruits are dark red and shiny, about one-half inch long with a thin skin covering a fleshy fruit. Each berry contains one or two large seeds (coffee beans). Processing the green beans takes expertise and, if done improperly, it detracts from the final product. The beans are shipped clean and dry to the coffee manufacturer where they are roasted and blended.

For convenience, ground coffee or coffee beans can be stored in the freezer in tightly sealed containers. Remove the needed amount and immediately return the unused portion to the freezer. Don't thaw and refreeze coffee. When grinding coffee, use a coarse grind for slow brewing and a fine grind for fast brewing.

Mountain Apple *Syzygium malaccense*

The mountain apple is oval, two to three inches long, and rather plump, with one or two large, brown seeds. The delicately flavored white flesh is crunchy, juicy, and pleasant. The tender skin varies from pink to scarlet or cerise. Wild mountain apples are especially refreshing to find and munch on a hike, especially on a warm day in Hawai'i.

The tree is native to India and Malaysia and found on many islands of the Pacific. In Hawai'i, it grows to about fifty feet and is found in backyard gardens and in valleys such as Sacred Falls (Kaliuwa'a) and Waimano Gulch near Pearl Harbor. In March and April, the tree, called 'ōhi'a 'ai, has showy, red-tufted flowers followed by fruit from July through December. There is a variety with white blossoms called 'ōhi'a kea.

Hawaiians opened the fruits and dried them in the sun. Although the fruit can also be dried today, if it is not consumed on the trail, it is best used in fruit and poultry salads or preserved as a sweet pickle.

'Ōhelo *Vaccinium reticulatum*

Hawaiians considered the 'ōhelo sacred to Pele, the volcano goddess, whose home was Kīlauea Crater. They threw offerings of 'ōhelo branches into the volcano pit before eating the berries until the kapu (taboo) was broken by high chiefess Kapi'olani in 1824.

The 'ōhelo is a member of the heath family and is related to the cranberry and blueberry. It is most abundant from June through September and is found on lava flows and cinder beds as well as on shrubland around Kīlauea Volcano and on the slopes of Mt. Haleakalā. The small shrub is one to two feet high, and round red or yellow fruit is about one-fourth to one-half inch in diameter with numerous small, flat seeds. Raw or cooked, the 'ōhelo makes a good sauce resembling a cranberry sauce. When served with ham or poultry, 'ōhelo is an unusual condiment.

Pohā   *Physalis peruviana*

The pohā, eaten long ago by Indian tribes in both North and South America, has many names, including Cape gooseberry, ground-cherry, husk-tomato, and strawberry tomato. It is called the Cape gooseberry because it was cultivated extensively at the Cape of Good Hope in the early nineteenth century. This member of the nightshade family was naturalized in Hawai'i before 1825 and can also be found growing wild in the hills of Sri Lanka, India, and the south of France. Pohā is grown commercially in Australia, New Zealand, and South Africa.

It is a perennial herb in the tropics, but an annual in temperate regions. In Hawai'i, it grows best on open mountain slopes between 1,500 and 4,000 feet. The plant is about two feet tall, with oval, velvety, heart-shaped leaves and yellow flowers. The edible, cherry-sized fruit has a thin, yellow-orange skin covering a spicy, juicy, tiny-seeded pulp. The fruit is encased in cream-colored parchment that resembles a miniature paper lantern. The lantern drops off before the fruit ripens to a bright orange. Green fruits are bitter.

Pohā can be adapted to most recipes calling for tart cherries or cranberry. It can be used for a fruit glaze on poultry or ham, for jam, or it can be puréed for puddings, ice cream, and cakes. Use it in stuffing, in a relish, or in muffins or breads. Dip pohā in chocolate and serve for dessert topping or garnish. The berries keep several weeks under refrigeration or can be frozen whole or puréed.

Tamarind   *Tamarindus indica*

The Arabs introduced tamarind, from the Arabic *tamrhindi* (Indian date), to Europe in the Middle Ages. It gives a sweet-sour, pleasant acidity to food, which has been described as refreshing. Don Francisco de Paula Marin supposedly planted the first tamarind trees in Hawai'i in 1797 at the corner of Booth Road and Huanu Street in lower Pauoa Valley on O'ahu.

The beautiful tamarind tree, graceful with feathery foliage and small red and yellow flowers, is a distant cousin of the string bean and a member of the pea family. In its native habitat of tropical Africa and southern Asia, it can grow to eighty feet, with a trunk size of twenty-five feet. In Hawai'i, it is a medium-sized tree.

The fruit of the tamarind is a pod three to six inches long, three-fourths inch wide, cinnamon-brown, and fuzzy. The pods hang in clusters on the tree.

The thick skin of the pod ripens to a thin, brittle, brown shell that does not open voluntarily. The shiny, brown seeds inside the pod are embedded in a jamlike pulp. When mature, the edible pulp shrinks from the pod. Dried tamarind is most commonly sold pressed into bricks called tamarind pulp or as a jellylike concentrate sold in jars. These are most likely to be found in Oriental or Indian markets. Tamarind purée is made from the concentrate and its fruity, sweet-sour flavor is widely used in Indian cuisine.

In Hawai'i, the fruit ripens during the late summer or early fall. The shelled fruit can be cooked until soft and then put through a coarse sieve to obtain as much pulp as possible. Use tamarind with water and a sweetener for a delightful beverage. The concentrate can tenderize meat or add zip to sauces, chutneys, and curries. It is used for a dipping sauce or drizzled over pastries.

'Ōhelo or Pohā Muffins

Yield: 1 dozen

1   cup whole-wheat flour

1/2 cup flour

1/2 cup regular rolled oats, uncooked

1/4 cup sugar

2   teaspoons baking powder

1/4 teaspoon salt

1/4 cup margarine

1   egg, beaten

1   cup skim milk

1   cup 'ōhelo or pohā berries, washed and coarsely chopped

1/2 cup pineapple tidbits, drained

1/4 cup minced crystallized ginger

Combine first six ingredients and stir well. Cut in margarine until mixture resembles coarse meal. Combine egg and milk. Add to dry ingredients, stirring to moisten. Fold in berries and pineapple bits. Lightly coat muffin pans with vegetable cooking spray. Spoon batter into prepared muffin pans. Fill to three-fourths full. Sprinkle crystallized ginger over muffin batter. Bake at 400° for 20–25 minutes or until done. Remove from pans immediately.

Sweet Pickled Wild Mountain Apple

Yield: 2 pints

3   pounds ripe wild mountain apples

2   cups white vinegar

1   cup water

1/2 cup sugar

1   cinnamon stick, broken into pieces

1   tablespoon ground mace

1   tablespoon allspice

1   tablespoon minced or grated fresh gingerroot

1   tablespoon whole cloves

Wash mountain apples, but do not peel. Cut them into halves, removing the blossom end, pit, and blemishes. Mix pickling ingredients in large pan over medium heat. Stir and bring to a boil. Add mountain apples and parboil until barely tender, about 30 seconds. Lift out the fruit and pack it into sterilized jars or freezer bags. Divide remaining liquid evenly among the containers. Cover immediately. Refrigerate or freeze up to 6 months. The flavor of the pickled fruit intensifies if refrigerated for 2 weeks before serving. These are especially good served with duck or chicken.

Spinach–Rice–Wild Mountain Apple Salad   Yield: 6 servings

12   wild mountain apples

2   cups cooked brown rice

3   tablespoons reduced-sodium soy sauce

1   teaspoon honey

1   tablespoon cider vinegar

1   teaspoon red pepper flakes

3   cups fresh, torn spinach leaves

1   cup thinly sliced fresh mushrooms

¼   cup thinly sliced celery

¼   cup thinly sliced green onion

Wash mountain apples, but do not peel. Cut them into quarters, removing the blossom end, pit, and blemishes. Place rice in large bowl to cool. Whisk together the soy sauce, honey, vinegar, and pepper flakes. Pour the mixture over the rice. Add all remaining ingredients, tossing gently. This salad can be refrigerated up to 8 hours before serving. The colors of cream, red, and green in this exotic salad make it a standout for buffet service.

Tamarind Chutney   Yield: approximately 5 cups

Both tamarind concentrate and dried pulp can be purchased at Indian or Asian specialty stores. To prepare tamarind from pods or pulp, soak the pulp in boiling water to cover and then pound lightly into a purée. Strain the purée to remove seeds and fiber. The strained pulp will resemble apple butter. Store in refrigerator. The concentrate is ready to use.

1   cup tamarind purée or ¼ cup tamarind concentrate dissolved in 1 cup water

¼   cup vinegar

3   cups firm papaya, mango, or pineapple chunks

½   cup minced gingerroot

¼   cup crushed red chili peppers

½   cup golden raisins or currants

¼   cup minced garlic

¼   cup honey

Bring tamarind and vinegar to a boil. Add fruit. Stir. Add remaining ingredients and simmer 15 minutes. Chill before serving. Or place into sterilized containers or freezer bags while chutney is hot. Cover immediately. Refrigerate up to 3 weeks or freeze up to 2 months.

Tamarind Ade

Yield: 4 servings

Place the contents of three or four tamarind pods, 5 cups of water, and ¹/₂ teaspoon honey into a sealed bottle. Shake. Refrigerate for 2 days, shaking the bottle occasionally. When ready to serve, strain and serve over ice. If using tamarind concentrate, dissolve it in water, allowing ¹/₂ teaspoon concentrate per serving, and adjust for sweetness. Serve over ice. Garnish with mint sprigs, a dash of ground cinnamon, or ground cloves. This invigorating drink and good thirst quencher is bottled commercially in some tropical countries.

Pohā Fruit Spread

Yield: 4 cups

Because pohā can be very tart, traditional preserves use 1 cup of sugar for every cup of fruit. The result is a thick, sweet spread that is mostly sugar syrup. This light pohā fruit spread is tart with a fresh fruit flavor. It is good on pancakes and waffles and as a glaze for lamb or poultry.

4¹/₂ cups pohā berries

1   cup fresh or frozen strawberry slices

1   package fruit pectin for light jam

4   tablespoons honey

Wash pohā berries and place in large saucepan. Lightly mash and cook over medium heat 3 minutes. Pour off liquid. Add strawberry slices, fruit pectin, and honey. Stir. Bring to a boil and cook 1 minute, stirring constantly. Remove fruit spread from heat. Pour into sterilized containers or freezer bags. Cover immediately. Cool at room temperature 24 hours and then refrigerate up to 2 months or freeze up to 6 months.

Pohā Relish

Yield: 2 cups

2 cups chopped pohā berries

2 cups chopped celery

1 cup chopped red apple

1/2 cup chopped sweet green pepper

1/4 cup walnut bits

1/2 cup cider vinegar

2 tablespoons brown sugar

1 teaspoon ground ginger

Combine all ingredients in 2-quart microwave-safe glass measure. Cook at High 5 minutes, stirring occasionally. Chill. Serve with turkey or ham. It can be used the same way as cranberry relish.

Pohā Stuffing

Yield: 5 cups

1 cup chopped pohā berries

1/3 cup chopped celery

3 tablespoons melted butter

1/4 cup mushroom pieces

3 cups herb-seasoned stuffing mix

2 cups cooked wild rice

1/3 cup nonfat chicken broth

1 teaspoon poultry seasoning

Combine all ingredients and stir well. This is especially good as a stuffing for Cornish game hen or lamb crown roast.

Kaua'i Mocha Muffins

Yield: 12 muffins

Celebrate the centennial return of the Kaua'i coffee crop to the marketplace with these rich, mocha muffins.

1¼ cups flour

¼ cup dark brown sugar

2½ teaspoons baking powder

½ teaspoon salt

½ teaspoon apple pie spice

½ cup chocolate morsels

2 tablespoons instant Hawaiian coffee granules

1 egg, beaten

1 cup Hawaiian coffee ice cream

⅓ cup cooking oil

Frosting:

1 (3-ounce) package cream cheese, softened

3 tablespoons coffee-flavored liqueur

¼ cup chocolate sprinkles

In a bowl, stir together the first five ingredients. Combine remaining muffin ingredients in a separate bowl. Stir chocolate mixture into dry ingredients to moisten. Lightly coat muffin pans with vegetable cooking spray. Fill prepared muffin pans two-thirds full. Bake at 375° for 20 minutes or until done. Cool muffins for 10 minutes in pan and then remove to wire rack.

To frost muffins, remove cream cheese from wrapper and place on micro-wavable plate. Microwave at High 30–60 seconds. Mix softened cream cheese with coffee liqueur. Spread frosting on muffin tops and decorate with choco-late sprinkles.

Flaming Coffee

Yield: 6 demitasse cups

3 cups hot coffee

⅓ cup brandy

1 tablespoon brown sugar

2 (3 by ¼-inch) strips orange peel

3 (2 by ¼-inch) strips lemon peel

2 teaspoons whole cloves

1 cinnamon stick, broken into pieces

Garnish: 2 tablespoons orange zest

Place hot coffee into a heat-resistant serving bowl. Combine remaining ingredients in a small, long-handled saucepan. Cook over medium heat until warm, but do not boil. The alcohol will evaporate if boiled. Ignite brandy mixture with a long match, taking care not to hover over the pan. Pour flaming brandy mixture over hot coffee and ladle into cups. Garnish with orange zest.

Nutritional Value of Fruits

Fruit (uncooked)	Serving Size	Wt. (g)	KCAL	Vit. A (IU)	Vit. C (mg)	Fiber (g)
Avocado	1 cup purée	171	370	1,407	18.2	4.85
Banana	1 cup mashed	225	207	182	20.4	1.40
Carambola	1 cup cubed	137	45	676	29.0	1.26
Cherimoya	1 fruit	547	515	55	49.2	12.03
Coconut	1 cup shredded	80	283	0	1.5	3.41
Grapefruit	1 cup with juice	230	74	286	79.1	0.46
Guava	1 cup	165	83	1,308	302.8	0.99
Jackfruit	100g	100	94	2.3	70.6	1.00
Kumquat	1 fruit	19	12	57	7.1	0.70
Lemon	1 medium fruit	58	17	17	30.7	0.23
Lime	1 fruit	67	20	7	19.5	0.34
Longan	1 fruit	3	2	—	2.7	0.01
Lychee	1 cup	190	125	—	135.9	0.39
Mammee apple	1 fruit	85	431	1,946	118.4	8.47
Mango	1 cup slices	165	108	6,425	45.7	1.38
'Ōhelo	1 cup	140	39	1,162	8.4	1.85
Orange	1 fruit	131	62	269	69.7	0.56
Papaya	1 cup cubed	140	54	2,819	86.5	1.08
Passion Fruit	1 purple fruit	18	0.13	126	5.4	1.97
Persimmon, Japanese	1 fruit	168	118	3,640	12.6	2.49
Pineapple	1 cup diced	155	77	35	23.9	0.84
Plantain (cooked)	1 cup	154	179	1,400	16.8	—
Pohā	1 cup	140	74	1,008	15.4	3.92
Pomegranate	1 fruit	154	104	—	9.4	0.31
Pummelo	1 cup	190	71	0	115.9	0.34
Sapodilla	1 cup pulp	241	199	145	35.3	3.37
Soursop	1 cup pulp	225	150	5	46.3	2.48
Star apple (caimito)	1 fruit	100	67	145	7.0	—
Sweetsop (sugar apple)	1 cup	250	236	15	90.7	3.68
Tamarind	1 cup	120	287	36	4.2	6.12
Tangerine	1 fruit	84	37	773	25.9	0.28

Abbreviations: g, gram; wt., weight; kcal, kilocalorie (the preferred and more precise form for calorie); IU, international unit; vit., vitamin; mg., milligram.

Fat content: coconut, 26.79 g; avocado, 17 g; macadamia nut, 98.79 g; Remaining fruits contain insignificant fat.

Source: U. S. Department of Agriculture, Agriculture Handbook 8-9. Composition of Foods, Fruits, and Fruit Juices, USDA, HNIS, 1982.

Information compiled by Joda Derrickson, M.S. R.D., Nutritional Specialist, University of Hawaii at Mānoa.

Bibliography

Asian Productivity Organization. *Fruit Production and Marketing in Asia and the Pacific.* Tokyo: Nordica International Ltd.,1985.

Bacon, Josephine. *Exotic Fruits A–Z.* Topsfield, Mass.: Salem House Publishers, 1988.

Bennett, Victor. *The Polynesian Cookbook.* New York: Galahad Books, 1974.

Clay, Horace Freestone. *The Hawai'i Garden.* Honolulu: University of Hawaii Press, 1977.

Frear, Mary Dillingham. *Our Familiar Island Trees.* Boston: Gorham Press, 1929.

Gast, Ross H. *Don Francisco de Paula Marin, a Biography:The Letters and Journal of Francisco de Paula Marin.* Edited by Agnes C. Conrad. Honolulu: University Press of Hawaii, 1973.

Gibbons, Euell. *Beachcomber's Handbook.* New York: D. McKay Co., 1967.

Grigson, Jane. *Exotic Fruits and Vegetables.* New York: Henry Holt Co., 1987.

Hamilton, Richard A. *Ten Tropical Fruits of Potential Value for Crop Diversification in Hawaii.* Research Extension Series 085. Honolulu: College of Tropical Agriculture and Human Resources, University of Hawaii, 1987.

Harris, Marilyn. *Mangos, Mangos, Mangos: Recipes and Art from Hawai'i.* Honolulu: The Printer, 1989.

Hawaii Agricultural Statistics Service. *Statistics of Hawaiian Agriculture, 1989.* Honolulu: Hawaii Department of Agriculture, 1990.

Heinz, Jenuwein. *Avocado, Banana, Coffee.* London: British Museum, 1988.

Jonas, Stephanie. *The Fruit Cookbook.* Frenchs Forest, N.S.W., Australia: Reed Books, 1985.

Krauss, Beatrice H. *Ethnobotany of Hawaii.* Honolulu:University of Hawaii Press, 1978.

Marcus, George, and Nancy Marcus. *Forbidden Fruits and Forgotten Vegetables.* New York: St. Martin's Press, 1982.

May, Ronald James. *Kaikai Aniani: A Guide to Bush Foods, Markets, and Culinary Arts of Papua New Guinea.* Bathurst, N.S.W., Australia: Robert Brown, 1984.

Miller, Carey D., Katherine Bazore, and Mary Bartow. *Fruits of Hawaii.* Honolulu: University of Hawaii Press, 1965.

Montagne, Prosper. *Larousse Gastronomique.* New York: Crown, 1961.

Neal, Marie C. *In Gardens of Hawaii.* Honolulu: Bishop Museum Press, 1965.

Morton, Julia F. *Fruits of Warm Climates.* Greensboro, N.C.: Media, Incorporated, 1987.

Oakman, Harry. *Tropical and Subtropical Gardening*. Milton, Queensland, Australia: Jacaranda Press, 1981.

Parkinson, Susan. *A Taste of the Tropics*. Alexandra, N.S.W., Australia: Prinut, 1985.

Rock, Joseph F. *The Indigenous Trees of the Hawaiian Islands*. Honolulu: Published privately, 1913.

Rosengarten, Frederic. *The Book of Edible Nuts*. New York: Walker, 1984.

Schneider, Elizabeth. *Uncommon Fruits and Vegetables: A Commonsense Guide*. New York: Harper & Row, 1986.

Siewertsen, Virginia, ed. *Citrus Fruits*. Kaua'i, Hawai'i: Na Lima Kokua, 1987.

Skinner, Gwen. *The Cuisine of the South Pacific*. Auckland: Hodder & Stoughton, 1983.

Sohmer, S. H. *Plants and Flowers of Hawai'i*. Honolulu: University of Hawaii Press, 1987.

Strauss, Sandra Conrad. *Fancy Fruits and Extraordinary Vegetables*. New York: Hastings House, 1984.

Tankard, Glenn. *Exotic Tree Fruit for the Australian Home Garden*. Melbourne: Thomas Nelson, 1987.

Wagner, Warren L., Derral R. Herbst, and S. H. Sohmer. *Manual of the Flowering Plants of Hawai'i*, 2 vols. Honolulu: University of Hawaii Press and Bishop Museum Press, 1990.

Wenkam, Nao S. *Foods of Hawaii and the Pacific Basin*. Honolulu: University of Hawaii, 1983.

Wenkam, Nao S. and Carey Miller. *Composition of Hawaiian Fruits,* Bulletin 135. Honolulu: University of Hawaii, 1965.

Wilder, Gerrit Parmile. *Breadfruit of Tahiti*. Honolulu: Bernice P. Bishop Museum, 1928.

Yardley, Maili. *Hawaii Cooks throughout the Year*. Hong Kong: Editions Ltd., 1990.

These tropical and rare fruit growers' associations publish newsletters and brochures giving gardening, recipe, and seed-sharing information:

California Rare Fruit Growers
Fullerton Arboretum
California State University, Fullerton
Fullerton, CA 92634

Hawaii Tropical Fruit Growers
P.O. Box 515
Kea'au, HI 96749

Rare Fruit Council International
P.O. Box 561914
Miami, FL 33256

Index

Sorbet: about, xiii–xiv; avocado, 8; banana–passion fruit, 21; carambola wine, 38; guava, 76; guava used in, 68; kumquat used in, 48; lemon used in, 42; lime used in, 44; passion fruit–lychee, 122; passion fruit used in, 120; pomegranate used in, 146; tangerine used in, 47

Soufflé: black sapote, 159; mammee apple, 159; sapodilla, 159

Soup: about fruit, xiii; avocado, xiii; breadfruit, 28; breadfruit used in, 24, 25; green mango used in, 93; green papaya used in, 106; guava, 70; guava used in, 68; lime used in, 44; papaya-chicken rice, 110; passion fruit, 120; persimmon, 126; pineapple, 126; plantain used in, 14, 15; pomegranate, 147; pomegranate used in, 146

Soups, 8, 9, 28, 70, 110, 120, 126, 147

Soursop. *See* Moya

Spread: about fruit, x–xi; carambola breakfast, 36; fruit, xv; guava, 73; mango, 99; mango-chocolate, 100; passion fruit, 122; passion fruit cheese, 128; persimmon, 127; persimmon cheese, 128; pineapple, 139; pohā, 167

Squash, acorn, orange, 57

Star apple, 156, 170

Star fruit. *See* Carambola

Stew: breadfruit used in, 24, 25; green papaya used in, 106; guava used in, 68; plantain used in, 14, 15

Strawberries, 56, 69, 74, 76, 117, 167

Strawberry tomato. *See* Pohā

Stuffing: macadamia, 88; macadamia nuts used in, 86; pohā, 168; pohā used in, 163; tangerine used with, 47

Sugar apple, 152, 170

Sweetsop. *See* Moya

Syrup: jackfruit used as, 154; pomegranate, 146

Tabbouleh: mango, 98; pineapple, 98

Tamarind, xi, xiii, xv, 31, 137, 163–164, 166, 170

Tangelo, 46

Tangerine, xi, xiii, xiv, 46–47, 50, 54, 55, 56, 58, 59, 82, 120, 159, 170

Tangor, 46–47

Tea, pineapple, 142

Thickener, use of avocado in soup for, 4; use of guava for, 68; use of plantain for, 14

Topping, 56; avocado used as, 3; banana, 16, 19; dehydrated mango used in, 93, guava used in, 69; macadamia nuts used in, 86; papaya, 114, 117; passion fruit, 123; passion fruit spread used as, 122, persimmon, 16; persimmon–peanut butter, 129; pineapple, 141; vodka citrus, 55

Turkey, with banana sauce, 17

Vegetable: coconut used with, 42; green papaya used as, 106; jackfruit used as, 154; lemon used with, 42; tangerine used with, 47

Vegetables, 8, 15, 25, 26, 27, 57, 59, 131

Vinegar: carambola, 36; carambola used in, 32; citrus, 52, 55; guava, 36; guava used in, 68; kumquat, 52; lemon, 52; lemon juice used as substitute for, 42; lime, 52; orange, 52; passion fruit, 148; passion fruit used in, 120; pomegranate, 148; pummelo, 52; rice, xv

Vodka, fruit, 55

Yogurt, persimmon, 126

Zest: about, xi; lemon, xii; lime, xii; orange, xii; tangerine, xii

About the Author

Marilyn Rittenhouse Harris, a longtime resident of Hawaii, received a B.S. degree from Purdue University and holds masters degrees from New Mexico University, the University of Southern California, and the University of Hawaii. She is the author of *Mangos, Mangos, Mangos: Recipes and Art from Hawai'i*, and her recipes appear frequently in newspapers and magazines. A former English teacher and librarian, Ms. Harris has taught tropical fruit cookery at Kapiolani Community College and the Lyon Arboretum. Her recipe for tropical peanut soup won the 1979 Christian Brothers Sherry–*Bon Appetit Magazine* Recipe Contest, and her chocolate chip cookie recipe appears in both *The 37 Best Chocolate Chip Cookies in America* and *The 47 Best Chocolate Chip Cookies in the World*. Her current research is on international foods and spices and the use of tropical fruits in Southeast Asia and the Middle East.

About the Illustrator

Charlene K. Smoyer is a graduate of Kamehameha School for Girls, the University of Hawaii, and the Artisan School of Interior Design. Her paintings have been exhibited in numerous shows and hang in many private collections. She is also a playwright whose works have been staged in Hawaii. Among her book illustrations are the pen and ink drawings for Marilyn Harris' *Mangos, Mangos, Mangos*. The illustrations for this book were drawn to actual size in Prismacolor (colored pencils). They are based on library, fruit market, and field research.